A TROWEL
AND
A SWORD

A TROWEL
AND
A SWORD

Prayer Practices for Those on
the Frontlines of the Gospel

VERLON FOSNER & JON DAVIS

Unless otherwise marked, Scripture quotations are taken from the New King James Version®. Copyright © 1982 by Thomas Nelson, Inc. Used by permission. All rights reserved.

Scripture quotations marked ESV® are from The Holy Bible, English Standard Version®, copyright © 2001 by Crossway, a publishing ministry of Good News Publishers. Used by permission. All rights reserved.

Scripture quotations marked NLT are taken from the Holy Bible, New Living Translation, copyright © 1996, 2004, 2015 by Tyndale House Foundation. Used by permission of Tyndale House Publishers, Inc., Carol Stream, Illinois 60188. All rights reserved.

Scripture quotations marked NIV are taken from the Holy Bible, New International Version®, NIV® Copyright © 1973, 1978, 1984, 2011 by Biblica, Inc.™ Used by permission of Zondervan. All rights reserved worldwide. www.zondervan.com The "NIV" and "New International Version" are trademarks registered in the United States Patent and Trademark Office by Biblica, Inc.™ All rights reserved worldwide.

Scripture quotations marked KJV are taken from the Holy Bible, King James Version, Cambridge, 1796.

Printed in the United States of America

Cover art by Nate Farro
Cover design and layout by Strange Last Name
Page design and layout by PerfecType, Nashville, Tennessee

Fosner, Verlon.
  A trowel and a sword : prayer practices for those on the frontlines of the Gospel / Verlon Fosner & Jon Davis. – Franklin, Tennessee : Seedbed Publishing, ©2021.

  pages ; cm .

  ISBN 9781628248890 (paperback)
  ISBN 9781628249019 (DVD)
  ISBN 9781628248906 (Mobi)
  ISBN 9781628248913 (ePub)
  ISBN 9781628248920 (uPDF)
  OCLC 1263877182

  1. Prayer--Christianity. 2. Prayer--Theology. 3. Holy Spirit.
  I. Title. II. Davis, Jon, 1959-

BV210.3.F67 2021   248.32   2021945186

SEEDBED PUBLISHING
Franklin, Tennessee
seedbed.com

I (Verlon) dedicate this book to my and Melodee's parents, who wrapped blankets around their shoulders and paced the floors in the early mornings of our family homes. They taught us what it looks like to "wait upon the Lord" and "pray the price."

I (Jon) am grateful for the opportunity to have a voice and speak into this project. I do so knowing that friends, family, mentors, and moments throughout my life have framed these thoughts. Two were crucial: my brother, friend, and lifelong mentor, Mike Atkins, who took me on and formed me for ministry and, most of all, my wife, Beth, who dared to love me more than I deserve and is an anchor and rock in my life every day.

CONTENTS

PREFACE

A significant portion of the Christian community holds a high view of God's sovereignty. Another portion of the family holds a high view of God's empowerment of the saints. In this book, two Christian leaders from both sides of the theological divide have come together to wrestle with the topic of spiritual warfare.

Doctor Verlon Fosner has served as a Pentecostal pastor with the Assemblies of God since 1981, and the Rev. Jon Davis PhD has served in ministry within the Episcopal Church both as a layperson and as a priest for most of his life.

Both authors wrestle to find common ground in the needed prayer-forms to pair with evangelism. Their efforts to articulate the differences serve as the backdrop of this reflection. It is both authors' hope that the readers of this book will find surprising insights from the healthy tension coming from the other side of the Christian family.

INTRODUCTION

The book of Nehemiah tells a story of a physical and spiritual restoration. It is a fairly quick read—thirteen chapters in the Old Testament—and would be a benefit to familiarize yourself with the story. Originally, the book of Nehemiah was combined with the book of Ezra; both speak to the rebuilding of Jerusalem, the temple, and the walls. Cities were defined by their walls as boundaries of protection. Without a wall, a city was vulnerable to siege and attack.

Nehemiah was called by God in a certain time to do a certain thing: to build a wall around Jerusalem to protect it from attack. Living in exile as the cupbearer to the king, a position of honor and trust, he heard of the situation in Jerusalem and he lamented, confessed, and repented. The king granted him favor and provision and Nehemiah set out on his quest to rebuild the walls of Jerusalem. Nehemiah is a study in leadership, and many have approached this text and narrative from that perspective. It is also a model for mission and prayer, and that is where we will dive headlong into these words.

Nehemiah was a practical man. He had a wall to rebuild, so he broke out trowels, put them into the hands of his workmen, and the wall began to take shape. Soon, however, the surrounding tribes began to threaten Nehemiah's workers because they did not want Jerusalem to regain their sovereignty, so he broke out swords and put them into the hands of his workmen as well. These swords were a practical response to the threats and serve as a great image and metaphor for prayer.

Churches that have not done the sociological work of learning how they can reach their neighbors and build the kingdom have no trowel in their hand. Thus, any conversation about picking up the sword of prayer is perhaps ill-timed. Similar to Nehemiah's story, spiritual opposition does not really manifest itself until a church starts turning sinners into saints in significant numbers. However, any church that does the missiological work of becoming effective in evangelism needs to be prepared for spiritual warfare. This group must learn to pick up the sword of prayer. Any group with an evangelism trowel in one hand and a prayer sword in the other is one powerful group. They know they are in a battle for the souls of people and are prepared to win it. Victory comes with the twofold work to defend and fight (the sword) and to build up, encourage, and sustain the mission (the trowel). Both are needed for mission advancement and success.

This is where I (Verlon) need to confess something. I was raised in a pastor's home where prayer was a very strong practice. In fact, the phrase "moving the hand of God" was as common around our dinner table as "please pass the potatoes." Even still, my ministry was more focused on practical leadership than prayer leadership. The fact that I am writing this book on prayer is probably a shock to those who know me. The reason I was so dulled by the idea of prayer wasn't that I disagreed with it theologically, but I was in reaction mode. Past generations have preached prayer, prayer, and more prayer and yet they were ineffective at evangelism, evangelism, and more evangelism. I found this disturbing. Thus, I did not want to be a part of another prayer effort that resulted in nothing more than creating a warm spiritual feeling among the saints, but without new people coming to Christ. But there came a day when my inattention to prayer exacted a certain price, and my awareness of the need for prayer changed—it changed with a jolt.

This book is for those who, like me, have been frustrated at the common understandings of prayer, and need to see a more practical approach—one that can actually turn a person's heart toward the Savior. These chapters are not something that can plug and play into any ministry story; rather, they provide an understanding of prayer for those who are intentionally and actively advancing the kingdom of God into the world one heart at a time. It is a vision of what happens when an effective prayer strategy pairs with an effective evangelism strategy, like Nehemiah's trowel in one hand and sword in the other. What follows is not the work of an academic theorist trying to advance truths from Scripture about prayer, but a ministry field commander who has encountered spiritual warfare and has returned from the frontlines to report that the swords found in the supply tents of the Holy Scriptures are sharp, effective, and necessary in the missional journey.

• • •

I (Jon) was invited into this space and structure that my friend Verlon has constructed. As I wandered through the prayer rooms he has described, I felt very much at home. I come from a different Christian heritage—liturgical, sacramental, and somewhat formal. It is a tradition rooted in prayer, so much so that we function with the *Book of Common Prayer*. I am a firm believer that next to the Holy Scriptures of the Old and New Testaments, the *Book of Common Prayer* is the second-best book we've got. I will pull a common thread throughout this collaboration from my prayer book background. I hope that in the same way the sword and trowel complement each other, Verlon's voice and my voice can do the same. There are many voices to consider—Scripture, church history, tradition, and the leading of the Holy Spirit. Our hope is that they will harmonize to form a symphony of prayer.

I don't just read prayers from a book. That is not my only frame of reference when it comes to prayer. I've led and participated in prayer meetings that spontaneously went on for hours. I've been on the frontlines of missional prayer to see a group of people, a church, a community, and even the nation and world transformed. I have a vocational track of more than thirty years of being engaged in youth ministry. I would often quote this same Nehemiah passage as the description of a youth pastor. We are to protect, defend, and fight for the souls of people with a sword in one hand *and* we are to build up and encourage, frame, and form individuals in faith. So, when I first engaged with this work it resonated deeply with me.

I expect you will hear two voices (maybe more) in these pages. That is a good thing. Being a musician, songwriter, and having recorded a few projects in my days, I appreciate harmony—intricate musical chords woven together to produce an inspiring sound. May you find some harmony between a Pentecostal pastor and an Episcopal priest as we seek to lend our voices, study, thoughts, experiences, and more to this needed area of discussion for the life and mission of the church.

I hear rumblings of a movement, a revival, and an awakening in these days. The church is in need of recapturing its missional posture. From a brief study of church history, we learn that every renewal, rebirth, restoration, and reformation was founded and rooted in prayer. We learn that behind every Luther, Calvin, Whitfield, Wesley, and Graham there was a sustained effort of missional, frontline prayer. Prayer is the fuel for mission; it opens doors, guides, breaks chains, and frees people to discover how great a salvation God has wrought for us in Christ.

Without another figure stepping in or on the horizon, I would propose the task of this missional work now falls on the local church. Rather than a crusade, the local church becomes the bearer of the gospel message to the world, and to do this it requires the same sort of prayer to sustain the mission.

1

PRAYER BILLABONGS

If we have no taste for the things of God, we can at least . . . ask for it, [and] it will be given us.

—THOMAS MERTON[1]

All prayer is beneficial, but not all prayer advances the mission of evangelism. Due to the urgency of seeking the lost, the prayer-forms that empower evangelism are held on a different level with a more pressing imperative than other practices. This is quite clear in the prayer Jesus taught His disciples where prayer for God's kingdom to come upon the earth preceded the prayers for provision, repentance, and even protection from evil. Many believers get so caught up in their personal issues that they never get back to "thy kingdom come."

In our current American version of Christianity, it is actually considered normal to focus our prayers on individual needs and spirituality. However, James 4:3

teaches that overly focusing our prayers on our own situations and desires is actually, "ask[ing] amiss" (KJV). To take this verse at face value suggests that much of our Christian culture needs to undergo a serious evaluation and adjust the disproportionate amount of our prayers that swirl around personal comforts like a billabong.

A billabong is an Australian term for eddies that form near the banks of a river. These little pools become separated from the stream and circle around and around at the river's edge. These waters are stale and can even become stagnated; they are waters that have seceded from the larger ecological system of rainfall creating headwaters, headwaters creating brooks, brooks draining downhill into streams, streams draining into rivers, rivers dumping into the ocean, oceans evaporating, evaporation seeding clouds, and, finally, the clouds releasing rain, which fills the headwater reservoirs again. Waters trapped in billabongs are disconnected from that eco-circle. Many prayer lives resemble billabongs because they are circling around and around in self-focused prayers that never seem to join the flow of God's great rescue mission for humanity. Let's discuss a few billabongs that are common in the American church.

Prayer Goal Confusion

Some Christians believe that prayer is primarily about talking to God and benefiting from that divine fellowship. And that is certainly an important aspect of a believer's prayer life. We glean and grow from time in

His presence. We tune our ears to the Shepherd's voice. We understand ever more deeply who we are in Christ as heirs, sons and daughters, soldiers, and more. I love this account regarding Mother Teresa. Dan Rather, CBS anchor, once asked Mother Teresa what she said during her prayers. She answered: "I listen."

So, Dan turned the question and asked: "Well, then, what does God say?"

Mother Teresa smiled with confidence and answered: "He listens." For an instant, Dan didn't know what to say. "And if you don't understand that," Mother Teresa added, "I can't explain it to you."

There is a place of deep connection and being still to know that He is God (see Psalm 46:10). Christian mystics abound throughout the ages and we have much to glean from writings and disciplines. A few throughout church history have had a very unique call to hide away in prayer and reflect on the Father, the Son, and Holy Spirit and we are richer for it.

However, there is another side to prayer that is sorely needed; this form of prayer is a gift that has been given so believers can download divine interventions onto the earth. Most Christians are comfortable with relational prayers that request things from a loving Father and edify the life of a Christ-follower. However, what is sorely needed is the form of prayer that opens big doors in heaven and advances the inbreaking kingdom of God upon the earth. There must be a time when we focus our prayers on the lost, the broken, and the people who cannot pray for themselves. Those who only bring personal prayers to the frontlines are akin to bringing a knife to a gunfight. It is a spiritual battle and one that we come to with weapons of warfare (see 2 Corinthians 10:3–6). Any Christian who cannot focus on that prayer goal needs to grow to become effective on the frontlines.

Prayer Tone Confusion

Another consideration has to do with the tone of our prayers. Frontline prayers are not relational as much as they are expectant. There are some who are concerned about prayers that sound like they are telling God what to do. And while there is a time to rest in the will of God, there is also a time to fervently seek God for the gospel effectiveness in our churches, neighborhoods, cities, and denominations. These prayers are not appeal-based prayers; they are declarative, bold, and expectant. We see this declarative form of prayer when Jesus taught the disciples to pray (see Luke 11:1–13). Notice the directness of Jesus' words: "Thy kingdom come. Thy will be done . . . Give us [this day] our daily bread" (vv. 2b–3 KJV). If Jesus' prayer had been appeal-based, it might have sounded like this: "Oh Father, please send Your kingdom upon us if it be Your will, and we ask that You provide for us the bread that we need today." But Jesus' instruction about prayer made no room for appeal-based words; He taught us to use declarative words. Then He immediately told a story about knocking on a neighbor's door with bold persistence until that neighbor gets up and gives you the bread that you need. He ended the story telling the disciples to pray that way, use that persistent tone, and expect it to work. In fact, Jesus spent three times as many verses teaching the expectant tone of prayer than He did teaching the actual words of prayer. And nothing in Jesus' prayer or follow-up instructional story made room for appeal-based prayers or tones. Jesus taught declarative prayers. We should learn to pray declarative prayers; we should learn to hold a cause-and-effect expectation in our souls; we should have a deep and abiding feeling that when we pray, something is going to happen.

These declarative prayers are always in agreement with Scripture. Here are a few:

> We destroy arguments and every lofty opinion raised against the knowledge of God, and take every thought captive to obey Christ, being ready to punish every disobedience, when your obedience is complete. (2 Cor. 10:5–6 ESV)

> I can do all things through him who strengthens me. (Phil. 4:13 ESV)

> For this reason, I remind you to fan into flame the gift of God, which is in you through the laying on of my hands, for God gave us a spirit not of fear but of power and love and self-control. (2 Tim. 1:6–7 ESV)

When we look through the Psalms, the Prophets, the Law of the Old Testament, the Gospels, the book of Acts, and the Epistles of the New Testament, we see this practice of making declarations, and as we fan the flame of declarative prayer, we do so aligned with what is declared in the very Word of God.

Declarative prayers open big doors for the lost and broken people we are sent to reach with the gospel. When it comes to evangelism, we do not pray passive prayers of appeal—we pray bold expectant prayers that flood the dark places in our towns with the light of heaven. We pray with boldness because the God-Family of the Trinity has put us on the earth for such a task as this. It might not be our nature to pray declarative prayers, but it is our calling. Let us not be confused about the prayers that are needed on the frontlines.

All Things Tend toward Entropy

Another billabong that the American church gets trapped in has to do with the tendency to drift away from the sacrificial forms of prayer in favor of the easy forms of prayer. Almost every Christian has at one time or another become inspired by a sermon, a scripture, or an evangelistic rally to pray for the lost in their city only to have their prayers for souls become reduced to inward concerns after a few days or weeks. The scientific law of entropy not only explains the degenerative elements at work in nature, it also explains degenerative spiritual practices like prayer. While most Christ-followers believe in praying for lost people to be brought to the Savior, the bulk of their prayers are focused on anything but. Author Mark Batterson wrote: "If we did an honest assessment of our prayer lives, I think we'd be amazed at the percentage of prayers aimed at *problem reduction*."[2]

One of the early church documents from the second century was the *Didache*. While this article was written during a season where several heresies were rising to threaten the purity of the faith, it is interesting to observe their focus on the inwardness of the church in their prayers: "Remember O Lord, Your church, save it from every evil and perfect it in Your love. Gather it together from the four winds and lead it sanctified into Your kingdom You have prepared for it."[3]

Within just a few decades, the church was seemingly showing signs of becoming self-protective and losing their preeminent cry for the sinner. If spiritual entropy could affect the first church, who lived within the near memory of the life of Christ, how much more might it affect those of us who are centuries removed from the life of Christ? None of us should be surprised when our prayer lives start swirling around our self-focused lives. However, this is one billabong we must swim out of, and get back into the flowing waters of God's inbreaking kingdom.

An aspect that can free us from prayer stagnation is to walk through the liturgical church year:

1) In the seasons of Advent, Christmas, and Epiphany, there is a movement from darkness to light: "The people who walked in darkness have seen a great light; those who dwelt in a land of deep darkness, on them has light shone" (Isa. 9:2 ESV). Each week in Advent it gets a little brighter. Christmas comes and the light of Christ enters

the world. Epiphany is the manifestation of the light of Christ to the whole world.

2) The seasons of Lent, Easter, and Pentecost follow a similar pattern, this time moving from death to life. In Lent we journey with Christ to the cross: to death, a body broken, and bloodshed. In Easter we rejoice at resurrection; death is conquered by the Christus Victor! In Pentecost there is a manifestation of this new and eternal life to the world by the coming of the Holy Spirit with power.

Whether in the church year or some other pattern, this movement and focus can deliver us from the entropy that paralyzes the prayer life of believers. Advent and Lent are seasons of preparation. Christmas and Easter are seasons of revelation and rejoicing. Epiphany and Pentecost are seasons of manifestation and the work of mission. This annual occurrence in the church calendar can be the needed focus to eliminate our stagnation.

A Hope and a Prayer

Another common weakening of a believer's prayer practice is when they view prayer as something they throw heavenward in hopes of gaining the attention of God. Christians who see prayer as a last resort after trying everything else have a defeatist view of prayer. These prayers are often used as a last resort when all else fails— like when a football team throws the Hail Mary pass into the end zone in the wild hopes that one of their players might catch it and win the game.

Kingdom prayer is nothing like that; kingdom prayers are a powerful activity that enables us to download the answers of heaven into the challenges of earth. Such a prayer-form is not based on a hope; it is based on a promise. Listen to the repeating refrains from this portion of Psalm 20:

> May the LORD answer you in the day of trouble!
> May the name of the God of Jacob protect
> you! ... May he grant you your heart's desire and
> fulfill all your plans! ... May the LORD fulfill all
> your petitions! ... he will answer him from his
> holy heaven with the saving might of his right
> hand. ... O LORD, save the king! May he answer
> us when we call. (vv. 1–2, 4, 5b, 6b, 9 ESV)

Talking to God about the needs of this broken world is far beyond a hope and a prayer; it is about urgency and intervention.

Generalized Prayer

Another element that diminishes the prayer efforts of a church is generalization. One pastor told a story of a special prayer meeting at his church. People were coming and going in their sanctuary in prayer shifts, when one man came in, walked to the front, kneeled at the altar, and prayed aloud: "Lord, save the whole world." Then he got up and walked out, feeling like he had done his part. While we might chuckle at that story, it resembles many forms of generalized prayer practiced by many today. Prayers like, "Lord, bring the unsaved into our church," serve as an example of generalization, and yet this is often the only form of evangelism prayer many believers know about.

The degeneration into generalized prayer started to affect the American church in recent decades as a natural result of the regional-church identity replacing the neighborhood-church identity. Throughout church history, local bodies of Christ commonly saw themselves as serving neighborhoods. It has only been in the last hundred years that the automobile changed walking cultures into driving cultures, which then changed our churches from neighborhood identities that served six-block walking circles into regional identities that served fifteen-minute driving circles. Then in the 1960s when the church-growth movement rose to dominance, the neighborhood-church identity became dismissed as an outdated form of church. However, the impact of this shift upon the mission and prayer of the church cannot be overstated. Neighborhood churches served their near neighbors, understood their needs, and prayed with specificity for their neighbors whom they knew by name.

After the birth of the regional-church identity, church families lost the close proximity to their neighbors, which had marked the church for nineteen hundred years. It is little wonder why prayer became diffused and confused, as there was no longer a particular neighborhood and specific neighbors for a congregation to focus their evangelism prayers upon. So, the prayer life of the believers began to mimic the regional identity of their church, and the result was generalized prayers over larger spaces that sounded like this: "Lord, send the lost to us." As well-meaning as these saints are who are praying for the faceless lost that live within a fifteen-mile circle around their church building, it is not the same as praying for Paul, Frank, Lisa, and Tina who live in the neighborhood. Dare I say, generalized and nameless prayers over large-scale areas avails little when compared to neighborhood-focused prayers. According to Alan Roxburgh, almost all of the stories in the New Testament occurred in the neighborhood.[4] Any group that feels sent to reach their neighborhood will find that generalized prayer for the lost will be replaced by a particular and impassioned prayer for their neighbors. And those prayers will avail much!

One of the rich treasures of the *Book of Common Prayer* is the breadth and depth of all the prayers offered. They are specific, tailored for exact and detailed situations. In the virtual world of Facebook, people will voice needs, concerns, and dire situations. Often, I (Jon) respond by posting a specialized prayer book prayer. Recently, a peer from college suddenly and unexpectedly passed away. He was in his fifties and it shook the community of his family and friends. I saw the post on Facebook and offered these from the Burial Service . . .

Into your hands, O merciful Savior, we commend your servant, Tom. Acknowledge, we humbly beseech you, a sheep of your own fold, a lamb of your own flock, a sinner of your own redeeming. Receive him into the arms of your mercy, into the blessed rest of everlasting peace, and into the glorious company of the saints in light. Amen.

Most merciful God, whose wisdom is beyond our understanding, deal graciously with Tom's family and friends in their grief. Surround them with your love, that they may not be overwhelmed by their loss, but have confidence in your goodness, and strength to meet the days to come; through Jesus Christ our Lord. Amen.[5]

Regardless of what we use when we lift our voices in a specific prayer for a specific situation, I believe God intervenes. One of the Fresh Expressions faith communities I am engaged with is a healing service at a local hospital. The service opens with a litany, which gives us focus. We then read a passage of Scripture followed by a reflection. Then we have a time of prayer. There are general prayers we pray as the Lord leads for the hospital, the staff, and the patients for peace, health, and wholeness. But then we engage in specific prayers for individuals and the unique situations they find themselves in. We get the details on someone's condition and the particular disease with which they are struggling. Something happens in that shift to a personalized prayer. Simply by mentioning someone's name, we get more connected as a community and are bound together in that moment as we engage for the sake of a named person.

Prayer Pride

Some individuals use prayer to prove how spiritual they are. Perhaps their need for validation gets in the way of actually moving the hand of God into the affairs of earth. Though someone can look like a spiritual giant when they pray, it can so easily be plain old-fashioned pride. Jesus saw this in His day in Matthew 6:5 and said that those who pray only to be seen and heard by others already have their reward. This is a sad verse to me. People who pray for reasons of recognition or pride will be ineffective in ushering God's plans on the earth. They will go through the mechanics of prayer, sacrifice time for prayer, and then only receive the reward of people praising them for their spiritual posture and well-worded prayers. Evangelism-birthing prayer and spiritual-looking prayer is not the same. Pride negates the results that prayer should be gaining and makes the time and sacrifice spent to be of little value in advancing the kingdom.

Every now and again I come across someone who announces that they are a prayer-warrior or an intercessor. Sometimes this makes me flinch because I sense that their self-ascribed title may be the only reward they will ever get. I know there are people who are actual prayer-warriors and intercessors—I have met them. True intercessors and prayer-warriors need no introduction because their esteem is not built by a title nor do they function in a way that others will see and admire their spirituality. Rather, they just do the hard work of downloading God's plans onto earth because they know they are called to do so.

It's interesting to note that when people in the Bible came into the manifest presence of God, there was a lot of falling down—Isaiah in his vision of the throne room of God, Paul on the Damascus Road, the apostle John in the book of Revelation, to name a few. We have access to God and can enter His presence boldly because of Christ. There is an intimacy we can have in our relationship with God. This speaks to immanence in that we can be close and near with no fear of the Almighty. As Romans 8:31–39 declares, we are fully reconciled and nothing can separate us from the love of God. In my (Jon's) tradition when we baptize, we make this pronouncement: "You are sealed by the Holy Spirit in baptism and marked as Christ's own forever." We are loved and cherished children and He is our Father, more so our Abba, which is best translated as Daddy or PaPa!

There is another issue: transcendence. God is holy, holy, holy. His thoughts and ways are higher; He is to be revered and honored. So, while we may enter His presence with boldness and confidence, we do so also with humility, awe, veneration, and amazement.

Liturgical worship can be rote and lifeless when simply going through a form. Yet liturgy can also be a vessel for the Holy Spirit to fill with power and presence. In the church, the overwhelming focus has been on the construct of immanence—God is my friend, my buddy, and pal. If this is the only side we embrace, we are out of balance; there must be both/and. We need the intimacy and the majesty, the boldness and the reverence.

The Silver Bullet

Another misstep that deserves mentioning is using prayer as the sole activity to reach the lost without viewing prayer as an important partner in evangelism. Prayer does not cancel the need for a church to do the missiological work of developing a viable redemption strategy. Prayer is not a silver bullet to get your church growing again. In fact, any group that asks God to answer their prayers but is not willing to answer His prayers that we engage with the lost is misunderstanding the nature of prayer. It is a two-way conversation that involves us inviting His kingdom to show up, and then offering our hands, words, time, and money when He does show up. Prayer that is not paired with a mission strategy is like a plane with only one wing.

Fifty years ago, our way of doing church was aligned closely enough to the sociology of our culture that prayer was all that was needed for God's kingdom to break into many people's lives. Today that is not the case. Timothy Keller reported that in earlier days you could afford to train people solely in prayer, Bible study, and evangelism—skills for their private lives—because they were not facing radically non-Christian values in their public lives.[6] However, now with the largest sector of our American population holding to a secular worldview, our evangelism prayers must be paired with some direct missional efforts on our part to do the work of reaching our neighbors. Prayer by itself, even powerful prayer meetings, is no longer a singular option that will compel the lost to run to Jesus.

I (Verlon) well remember a conversation with a pastor in our nation who epitomized my frustration with prayer as commonly practiced. He reported that his church had been stalled for many years. So he focused his church on prayer with the hope that it would reenergize their evangelism. He scheduled prayer teams, called prayer events, took his people to prayer retreats, invited prayer teachers to deepen their understanding, and even built a prayer tower on their property. He continued this prayer campaign for several years. Then he turned to me and said, "Verlon, do you know what all of this prayer did for us? Nothing!" After all of that effort, they had the same exact people and the same exact attendance. He went on to say that they canceled their prayer initiative as ineffective. Then he said something I will never forget: "It broke my heart that all of our thousands of hours of prayer did not work better than that." His story and his honesty captured my attention. There is no powerful future for people who are willing to pray for the lost, but are not willing to offer themselves to be a part of the missional answer. In this day, prayer is not a stand-alone silver bullet to get our churches growing again.

In Holy Week of 2019, Notre Dame Cathedral in Paris caught fire and burned. The world watched in amazement. People in Paris filled the streets and watched this monument and landmark be reduced to ashes. I (Jon) watched the news and was taken aback by the fact that people noticed a church on fire. That has not happened in a while, especially in Europe. There are exceptions, but in Europe, for the most part, churches tend to be museums people visit.

The world has changed. We find ourselves in an uncharted territory in the twenty-first century of post-Christendom. There is much to lament regarding the immorality that is now accepted and even celebrated. Western culture is adrift in a sea of relativism and subjectivism fueled more intently in the last decade by social media. What can move us forward away from the billabongs and back into the flow? I am convinced missional frontline prayer will be the means by which we see true revival and reformation.

Verlon is right-on in this call to evangelism. I often think of evangelism as that moment when I get to pray with someone to know Jesus, to lead them in a sinner's prayer of faith and repentance. Evangelism is so much more. To use an agrarian metaphor: the ground is tilled, the soil prepared, seeds are sown, a crop is watered and nourished, shoots sprout up, and, finally, there is fruit. All of these steps are necessary to bring in a harvest.

God is at work in a person's life long before that moment of praying a prayer to come to Christ and become a new creation. God is orchestrating the process from beginning to end and He wants to use us, the church, as instruments in His hand to engage people, love them as Christ does, and sow seeds with thought, comments, and especially good questions. I've been in and participated in every stage of evangelism. I've had the opportunity to be in the moment of gospel harvest many times. But I always remember that there was a lot of work and prayer done before that prayer of salvation was prayed.

Dan Kimball states: "The constant thread in the early church was prayer."[7] Our prayers, like the saints who have gone before, are supposed to be the thing that opens the door for God to change our world. When prayer is envisioned in any other way, it will be trite. Michael Slaughter states: "The enemy's purpose is to distract us to a lower level of living until we die."[8] Believe it or not, prayer meetings can be done in such a way that they are lower-level events. And they pale in comparison to the fiery evangelism prayers of the early church in Acts 4:31, where after they prayed the meeting place shook. It is possible that their prayers were so voluminous and energetic that it rattled the rafters, but because the verse states that the shaking occurred after they prayed it is more likely that it was a divine demonstration that God was moving quickly, actively, and rambunctiously to respond to their prayers.

Ignoring Spiritual Realities

In the age of enlightenment, we can seem dismissive of the supernatural. This is another billabong to be sure. We analyze, explain, and justify things by the scientific method. I am all for science and what it has taught us about the world. I have to believe if you are reading this you are also a person of faith knowing that all we see is not all there is. I don't want to delve into all of the mysteries of faith and Scripture. I do believe the Word of God is true and as Article Six of the Thirty-Nine Articles states:

> Holy Scripture containeth all things necessary to salvation: so that whatsoever is not read therein, nor may be proved thereby, is not to be required of any man, that it should be believed as an article of the Faith or be thought requisite or necessary to salvation. In the name of the Holy Scripture we do understand those canonical Books of the Old and New Testament, of whose authority was never any doubt in the Church.[9]

I would also approach this from a creedal perspective. I believe that Apostles' and Nicene Creeds state true Christian faith and this is what a Christian believes. As related to Scripture, it is an absolute that God created this world. Was it accomplished in six, twenty-four-hour days? Or are the days mentioned segments of time beyond what we understand? There is room for interpretation on this; we may disagree on the how of creation, but I still believe the essential tenets of the creeds—I believe in God the Father, Maker of heaven and earth. My point would be as we look at a biblical warrant for spiritual warfare, we might interpret the material differently at times, but we will all see the presence of spiritual realities.

A quarter of Jesus' ministry dealt specifically with conflict between the kingdom of God and the dominion of darkness and evil. The very incarnation of Christ was the beginning of an assault on Satan's domain. Jesus came to crush Satan under His feet. Jesus begins His ministry, immediately following His baptism by John in the Jordan River, by being led by the Spirit into the wilderness where He would fast for forty days and be tempted by the devil. In this spiritual warfare, Jesus uses Scripture as His response to what the devil was offering and He emerges victorious from this wilderness journey.

There are multiple instances of demonic deliverances throughout the Gospels. In these accounts, the demons declare who Jesus is, submit to His authority, and recognize their defeat. We cannot ignore these stories and teachings simply because we are living in an age of rationalism. All that being said, the biblical picture is not one of dualism. We are not in *Star Wars* dealing with equal parts of the Light Side and the Dark Side of the Force. Thankfully, our God is omnipotent and omniscient—He is all-powerful and all-knowing. Satan and the forces of evil are not.

In the story of Job in the Old Testament we are given an account where God is proud of His servant Job and Satan challenges God that Job is only good because God had blessed him! God permits Satan to wreak disaster on Job's life, destroying his family, taking his wealth, and then inflicting him with disease. Satan could not do this without God's permission. God is not the cause of evil; He is holy and righteous.

I don't have the space here to deal with all the issues of providence, sovereignty, and the problem of evil in this world. We can say that Jesus came to establish the kingdom of God, to defeat Satan, and to redeem us from sin. Mike Atkins, my lifelong friend and mentor, once explained it this way:

> People ask: "If God is good, then why is there evil in this world?" Be assured God will judge every evil act. Every violence, murder, thievery, atrocity. All the evil in the world is being recorded and there is a day of judgment coming. It is time that is posted on God's eternal calendar. God will pour out His wrath against sin and His justice will prevail.

There was also a day of judgment two thousand years ago when Jesus was nailed to the cross and took upon Himself the burden of all the evil that had been and would be committed. "For our sake he made him to be sin who knew no sin, so that in him we might become the righteousness of God" (2 Cor. 5:21 ESV). The good news is that we choose which day of judgment we will be under. Will we stand alone before almighty God, giving an account for our lives, knowing that if we are guilty of one infraction—one lie, one evil thought—we are guilty of breaking all of the law; or will we put our faith in Jesus, repent of our sin, and believe in Him to be our Savior and Redeemer.

There is a widely held view regarding the consummation of the kingdom of God and the second coming of Christ rooted in a metaphor of D-Day and VE-Day. On June 6, 1944, when the Allied invasion of the European continent was successful, the war was over. Germany had lost and they could not stand against the wave of military that would flow all the way to Berlin. However, there would be some eleven months of battles, destruction, and thousands of lives lost until Germany would surrender on what became known as Victory in Europe Day, May 8, 1945. The cross of Jesus and His resurrection were a D-Day moment. Satan was utterly and completely defeated. Jesus was the Christus Victor! The consummation of God's kingdom at the return of Christ will be like a VE-Day. Until then, we live in an in-between time of the "already" and "not yet." Victory in Christ is ours. In the spiritual sense, we possess everything necessary as kingdom people, heirs and joint heirs, redeemed, reconciled, and made righteous in Christ. However, in this season we still have spiritual warfare; there are battles to be fought, casualties, and destruction. Yet we fight on, knowing of an assured victory in Jesus.

We have instruction to put on the whole armor of God and, having done all, to stand against the fiery darts of the devil (see Ephesians 6:10–18). We are also told that our warfare is not fleshly but rather divine, destroying strongholds of the enemy (see 2 Corinthians 10:3–6). Again, we are warned: "Be sober-minded; be watchful. Your adversary the devil prowls around like a roaring lion, seeking someone to devour" (1 Peter 5:8 ESV).

Missional, frontline, trowel-and-sword prayer is grounded in spiritual warfare. It is fulfilling a first-commission mandate, found in Genesis 1:28 (ESV):

And God blessed them. And God said to them, "Be fruitful and multiply and fill the earth and subdue it, and have dominion over the fish of the sea and over the birds of the heavens and over every living thing that moves on the earth."

In Luke 10, Jesus sends out seventy-two of His followers and disciples on a mission. It is a central narrative to how we understand the mission of the church today. They return, rejoicing, and we have this account:

The seventy-two returned with joy, saying, "Lord, even the demons are subject to us in your name!" And he said to them, "I saw Satan fall like lightning from heaven. Behold, I have given you authority to tread on serpents and scorpions, and over all the power of the enemy, and nothing shall hurt you. Nevertheless, do not rejoice in this, that the spirits are subject to you, but rejoice that your names are written in heaven." (vv. 17–20 ESV)

These words of Jesus are important for so many reasons. While there is an over-focus in some corners on spiritual warfare and demonic activity, what I hear in this passage is the power of evil is to be contended with and confronted. While we contend with evil in order to advance the kingdom, our loud rejoicing is reserved for what Christ Jesus has done for us! So, as we go forward into the chapters before us, may we never forget to rejoice over the "already" more than we contend for the "not yet." This is Jesus' directive to us all.

2

EFFECTIVE EVANGELISM AND THE SUBSEQUENT WAR

> There is only one kind of violence that captures the Kingdom of Heaven. . . . the seeming violence of grace, which . . . sets order in the house of the soul.
>
> —THOMAS MERTON[1]

(Verlon) could not believe what I was hearing on the phone from one of our state agencies. Our forty-year-old childcare was being pulled into a complicated court case that was forcing us to close our doors unless we could post one hundred thousand dollars for legal fees. We did not have anything close to that. Within the month, we were laying off nineteen employees and sending fifty-five families searching for new childcare. As difficult as it was to say goodbye to this wonderful ministry and the team that ran it, it was also difficult to replace the significant amount of finances that had been flowing from that childcare and funding several of our new churches. These are the things pastoral nightmares are made of. And though we were exonerated legally, we were not able to restore the ministry financially. It took the wind out of our financial sails, to say the least. However, it did not destroy us. Rather, it did something remarkable in us: it taught us a depth of prayer that we had never experienced before.

We had been a traditional Seattle church who started to decline in 2004. After much soul-surgery, we felt directed by the Lord to go back to doing church like church was done primarily throughout the Apostolic Era—the Agape Feasts, in which church was done around tables filled with food. We resisted for a season because we really liked our Sunday morning church, but we ultimately yielded to the Spirit's direction and started doing church around tables in community spaces in Seattle neighborhoods. Immediately, our rooms began to fill up with more non-churched people than we had seen in decades. We became so effective at bringing lost people to Jesus at our dinner churches that, after eight years, we had fully transitioned into a multisite dinner church, serving Jesus dinners in a different neighborhood every night of the week and *influencing three times more people each week than our congregation had ever served throughout its history.* We were making plans to open our ninth site and had never felt so effective in evangelism. And then came the legal action that kicked in the front door of our house.

Effective in the Mission

Becoming effective in evangelism is not an easy thing to do. As previously stated, it is not achieved by prayer alone, but rather by doing the hard work of missiology. There is a potent primary question leaders and churches must ask themselves if they desire to become effective in evangelism: Who are we supposed to rescue next? Every group must come to a point where they feel sent by the Lord to rescue a particular under-gospeled people circle. It might be an isolated population or a particular under-churched neighborhood. While under-gospeled might be a cumbersome phrase, it is an important one because our towns are filled with circles of people who gather for all kinds of reasons; it is into these circles of people that leaders can incarnate and, in time, raise up a new faith community. The idea of mission is frustrating until you know who you are called to reach. Further, it's worth noting that there is a good chance that your effective evangelism story will begin where human need is the greatest, perhaps in a challenged neighborhood near you. In other words, when a group pauses to ask Jesus *who* He wants them to rescue, it is likely their eyes will become open to a nearby neighborhood where isolated, broken, and ruined lives are most present.

A second question a church must ask themselves to enter into effective mission is: How do we do church for the people we are sent to and how do we do it in a way that fits their sociology? This, too, is a huge question and requires leadership boldness to repeatedly ask until a different vision of doing church emerges. Everyone knows how to do church for the already saved; we have been doing that for five hundred years. But that history, however meaningful it is to us, does not help a people group to which we might be sent. Note: if our traditional way of doing church fit the sociology of these neighbors, they would have already joined us. Their absence makes it clear that our Sunday gatherings do not fit their realities; we must listen to what the under-churched neighborhoods are saying to us.

Once a church answers both of those questions effectively and stops insisting on the manner of church that they like, their evangelism effectiveness will probably start to soar. And it is a beautiful thing to be working on the rescue mission beside the Rescuer—Jesus Himself. But beware: as steep of a hill as it is to become effective in evangelism, the steepest climb awaits.

It was 1996, and I (Jon) was leading some national youth ministry efforts within the Episcopal Church. We were in a stretch where a national youth conference had taken off and a couple of thousand Episcopal youth gathered each year to hear the gospel and grow in their knowledge and love for Christ. This was also a season of great conflict in the church over issues that later would birth deep schism. It seemed that one of the things the conservative branch was doing and doing well was youth ministry.

A national leader representing an organization came to our youth ministry coalition and asked us to put on a youth event. (Ultimately, it was intended for a political agenda, to make a statement about the good work of youth ministry.) We were asked to do a youth mission and outreach to coincide with a national Episcopal event. It felt like this authentic and deeply blessed work, birthed by the Holy Spirit, was being extorted for political purposes. I entered that meeting knowing I had to say what was on my heart, and I did. After hearing the proposal and invitation, I immediately piped up and said, "I don't mean any disrespect, but we cannot put on a youth event, mission, or outreach unless God has told us to do so and, more so, that He has broken our hearts for the people we are going to serve." My comment essentially ended the conversation and we did not participate.

When God has a people group for you to reach, He will show you and you will become burdened for them with a divine empathy. I have consistently seen this occur in friends of mine for international students at a university, athletes, people in needy neighborhoods, the persecuted church, and human-trafficked populations. I know people who have given their lives and resources to minister in these and countless other groups.

Recently, I got involved in a homeless breakfast church in downtown Orlando. I was asked to fill in, play some music, and share a message. I showed up at 6:00 a.m. and I watched as about two hundred street people filed in, respectfully took their place, were served coffee, and sat through the music and message. I have since been back to be a part of this community; I am burdened for them and pray for the Good News Breakfast daily.

Answering the questions Verlon proposed is essential for godly mission; they develop a motivation to love broken, wounded, captive, and lost people. We might get an invitation and a door may open, but what drives us is a passion for those who are currently outside of the household of faith to be drawn into the kingdom of Christ.

Counterattack

It is usually assumed that effective prayer will precede effective evangelism. While prayer anytime is better than prayerlessness, I would offer a different progression. In Nehemiah's story, they were effectively rebuilding the wall around Jerusalem when the attacks started. These threats are what prompted them to pick up the sword. Our Seattle story followed that same trajectory; we had become effective at rescuing the lost in the isolated neighborhoods of our city when the spiritual attack came. In reality, it was a counterattack—we were the ones who had drawn first blood.

Matthew 12:29 makes it clear that any effectiveness in reaching the lost is actually plundering the strongman's house. Our evangelism efforts were actually rescuing oppressed people out of captivity and darkness. Thus, our success was nothing short of plundering the enemy's house, and that prompted his counterattack. We see this same pattern in Luke 10:18 when Jesus sent out the seventy-two disciples to heal the sick and announce the new kingdom of God. Afterward, they returned excited about their gospel success, to which Jesus told them He saw Satan fall from the sky like lightning. In other words, Satan was losing place; his house was being plundered. But for us, this victory was short-lived, because a counterattack was coming.

The night of the Last Supper, Jesus took His disciples into the garden of Gethsemane to pray. There, Jesus was in anguish over the suffering coming His way; His stress was so great that drops of blood seeped out of His pores and ran down His face. The disciples slept as Jesus prayed—in many ways abandoning Jesus when He needed them most. Then adding to the insult was Judas's kiss and betrayal, which brought about an arrest in the dark of night.

All of this was a satanic counterattack that was being waged against the kingdom of God. This is made clear in Luke 22:53 when Jesus said, "This is your moment, the time when the power of darkness reigns" (NLT). Jesus' evangelistic success brought on a certain counter-attack from Satan. This is the nature of spiritual warfare; a back-and-forth battle is being waged. Wonderfully, it would end in the defeat of Satan and all the powers of darkness at the cross.

Similarly, every servant since the example of Christ who has become effective at advancing the gospel has met the same result. The strongman does not like his house being plundered, and he will mount a counterattack. In Ephesians 6:16 we are told: "In all circumstances take up the shield of faith, with which you can extinguish all the flaming darts of the evil one." The devil will throw all manner of flaming darts to distract us and hinder the gospel mission. Yet we have a sure defense when we trust and believe. Once we understand this, our prayer lives change forever.

When we step up and step out into a missional work, we do so in a posture that is somewhat exposed, transparent, and vulnerable. By simply saying yes to a call and starting a new initiative, we can become a target. "Fear not" is the most common exhortation in the Scriptures—and it usually precedes a call to action. Accordingly, we fear not because we have a victory, we have spiritual weapons to advance the work, we have armor to cover our exposure, and we know how the story ends!

Rampant Burnout

Leaders are leaving the ministry in record numbers today. Jim Cymbala reports that across America, fifty leaders per day are resigning their post, mostly due to burnout.[2] Congregants are quitting their volunteer positions after only a few months of service in increased numbers, citing burnout as their reason. While there are several causes of burnout, the primary reason in my view is a lack of success in the gospel mission. Leaders and volunteers thrive when they see that their work is making a difference. But we live in a church world where declines are more normal than successes. Eighty-five percent of US churches are stalled and in decline.[3] And according to Andy McAdams, an unfathomable 99 percent of churches cannot replace their attrition by reaching the lost.[4] The small percentages of churches that are growing are doing so from transfer growth. The vast majority of our churches across all denominational lines are wholly ineffective and under-practiced at reaching lost people in their community, which makes the future of their church unsustainable. It is little wonder why pastoral burnout has reached chronic levels.

Twenty-three years ago, this was a perfect description of my (Verlon's) ministry. I was ineffective at both the trowel and the sword. My struggle got so bad that I dipped into a clinical depression. The metaphor often used to define clinical burnout is being in a boxed canyon and bumping against the rock wall at the end of that canyon so many times that your emotional reservoirs empty out and you are forced to give up. That was my reality; I knew I was called to reach the lost in my city, but I didn't know how. And after fifteen years of failing, my soul had given up on me.

Now, I sit in a chapter of my ministry where I have learned how to be effective at reaching the lost in my city. However, I am watching throngs of ministers and volunteers in congregations around me burning out from a sense of failure as their church continues to decline year after year. This saddens me beyond words. To be ineffective at both the trowel and the sword is a fast path to discouragement and depression. While there is a new chapter coming to the American church, for the present it is statistically obvious that the strongman is maintaining an upper hand over the mission of the church. This must change!

I (Jon) was told early on as I considered a vocational call to ministry: "If you can do anything else and be happy, then do it! If you can't, then you are discerning a call to ministry." As my friend Steve Brown quips, "I have been a professional religious person for most of my life." This adage is surely true for me. In these many years I have experienced great successes and a few failures; there has been a lot to celebrate and there have been many dark nights of the soul. What has sustained me in the good, the bad, the ups, and the downs is an ever-growing relationship with the Lord that is anchored in prayer.

I have discovered (and rediscovered) time and again that I cannot give away what I do not have. If I want the flock I am shepherding or the ministry I am leading to be missional and serious about advancing the gospel, it begins with me. Ministry competence is not found in simply reading theology or being awarded positions or degrees. It comes in the pastoral trenches in a posture of prayer that restores our souls for His name's sake, grows a holy relationship, and creates a fresh wind that advances the kingdom into the world.

This Is War

In this day of salvation, we have all been born into a perpetual spiritual conflict. The servants of Christ are called to rescue the perishing from the strongman's house, and the strongman will assuredly attack back. It does us well to admit the contentious nature of spiritual things upon the earth. Satan's kingdom with his oppressive plans is at work, and God's kingdom with His beneficial plans is also at work. And they are both focused on the same thing: humanity. It is difficult for most people to hear that we live in a battleground. The idea of peace is far preferred by most personality types, and yet peace is not the order of the day in which we live. Any leader or Christ-follower that longs to rescue the lost must realize that they will enter into a war zone to fulfill that longing. Prayer takes on an entirely new nature in the war zone from the prayers that were practiced in the safe zones. Many people's prayer lives are shallow for the simple reason that they have never been invited into the calling of evangelism and its war zones. Their prayers are for their problems, their wants, their family, their church, and their friends. But let that same person become emotionally invested in someone's life being destroyed by the works of the devil, and their prayer life will deepen as they begin to contend for the soul of that friend.

The apostle Paul knew the battlefield well. His counsel in Ephesians 6:12 to all who would be advancing the gospel behind him is that we actually "wrestle" against principalities, against powers, against the rulers, against darkness, against spiritual hosts, and against wickedness. What a great description of the hand-to-hand combat we should expect to encounter if we enlist in the God-family rescue business. We are at war! The prayers that are practiced in war zones are very different than the prayers we use for ourselves. But do not fear—winning these wars is exactly what the Christian life is designed for.

I like Verlon's war-zone picture as it calls us to action. There is an image of Jesus that is accurate, tender, kind, compassionate—Jesus, meek and mild. There is also a fierce and powerful Jesus who worked hard in a carpenter's trade and who took a whip and overturned tables in the Jerusalem temple. I need both in my life. There are either/or moments in life when we have to make a choice. When it comes to mission and ministry, the more we can do both/and, the better; old and new, truth and grace, make for an expansive landscape. Trowel-and-sword prayers reflect these two positions. The trowel is there to build; the sword is there to fight.

There is a picture from church history that speaks to this war-zone posture: *rogation*. Rogation comes from the Latin and simply means "to ask." The church at the beginning in the fifth century set aside days in the church calendar to ask for God's blessing and protection, specifically on the land itself. This was in an agrarian society, so during the days of spring the local clergy would bless the ground for farming, the seeds for sowing, the implements employed, the people and animals for working, all in hopes of a bountiful harvest come fall. As we moved from an agrarian existence, prayers were added to bless business and industry.

There was a focus on true repentance in rogation, which has less to do with spiritual morality and more to do with aligning ourselves with the ways of God. To repent is to turn around. In a spiritual sense it is to acknowledge that living by our own wits and ways is not healthy and we need to learn to walk in God's ways. We turn toward the Lord. We have the pronouncement of absolution from the *Book of Common Prayer*: "Almighty God, our heavenly Father, who of his great mercy has promised forgiveness of sins to all those who with *hearty repentance* and true faith turn unto him."[5]

Thus, repentance was eagerly and energetically sought; this was a solemn and revered prayer. So serious was the repentance that it turned into joyful resolve; it was a spiritual decision that demanded a celebration!

Associated with rogation was a service of Beating the Bounds. This was marked by a procession throughout the community in which the participants took spiritual authority over the elements of darkness. It was, to quote Verlon, "a frontlines prayer-form; hand-to-hand combat advancing the cause of the kingdom." This has long been the posture of the church. In the Beating of the Bounds, this procession might employ the Great Litany as a pattern for their prayer. Here are some excerpts: (The whole of the Great Litany is in appendix 2.)

> Remember not, Lord Christ, our offenses, nor the offenses of our forefathers; neither reward us according to our sins. Spare us, good Lord, spare thy people, whom thou hast redeemed with thy most precious blood, and by thy mercy preserve us forever,
> *Spare us, good Lord.*

> From all evil and wickedness; from sin; from the crafts and assaults of the devil; and from ever-lasting damnation,
> *Good Lord, deliver us.*

> From all blindness of heart; from pride, vain-glory, and hypocrisy; from envy, hatred, and malice; and from all want of charity,
> *Good Lord, deliver us.*

From all inordinate and sinful affections; and from all the deceits of the world, the flesh, and the devil,
Good Lord, deliver us.

From all false doctrine, heresy, and schism; from hardness of heart, and contempt of thy Word and commandment,
Good Lord, deliver us.

From lightning and tempest; from earthquake, fire, and flood; from plague, pestilence, and famine,
Good Lord, deliver us.

From all oppression, conspiracy, and rebellion; from violence, battle, and murder; and from dying suddenly and unprepared,
Good Lord, deliver us.

By thine Agony and Bloody Sweat; by thy Cross and Passion; by thy precious Death and Burial; by thy glorious Resurrection and Ascension; and by the Coming of the Holy Ghost,
Good Lord, deliver us.

In all time of our tribulation; in all time of our prosperity; in the hour of death, and in the day of judgment,
Good Lord, deliver us.

That it may please thee to bless and keep all thy people,
We beseech thee to hear us, good Lord.

That it may please thee to send forth laborers into thy harvest, and to draw all mankind into thy kingdom.
We beseech thee to hear us, good Lord.

The Intimidator

Satan does not have superior power. While this will be discussed at greater length in the next chapter, for now 1 John 4:4 states that greater is He who lives in you than he who lives in the world. Satan may be able to bring some dark clouds over our lives for a season, but he cannot attack and overpower us with brute strength for unlimited seasons. That should serve as a confidence builder to anyone following Christ into the rescue mission.

Given his inferior power to that of Christ and Christ's servants, our enemy tends to use a strategy of intimidation. We see this in Nehemiah's story when the neighboring towns that opposed the building of the wall had some of their people begin yelling at the workmen on the wall while rattling their weapons and promising to attack if the men kept working. Operation Intimidation was officially launched.

Today, Operation Intimidation comes mostly in the form of inward fear; Satan works very hard to keep Jesus' people afraid of something. In 1 Peter 5:8, the apostle Peter recognized this intimidation strategy: "Your adversary the devil walks around *like* a roaring lion, seeking whom he may devour" (emphasis added). It is true that Satan looks to devour and oppress people, which is the exact reason why serious Christ-followers enter the battle in the first place. However, when that lion roars at us, he is hoping to inspire fear and intimidate us to back out of the war zone and leave him to devour others at will. As tempting as it might be to avoid conflict with the enemy, we need to know that he is not actually a lion; he can only stomp around and roar *like* a lion. Look again closely at the verse. He's like a lion, but he is not a lion. The only actual lion on the earth is the Lion of Judah, which is Jesus, and He lives in us. Because we have the *actual* lion living within us, each one of us is more lion-like than Satan can ever be. Once we learn the truth of his false roar and our actual roar, the war changes forever. We must remember we are lions, pray like we are lions, act like we are lions, and stay in the fight like a lion would. In 2 Timothy 1:7 (ESV) Paul was trying to help his young protégé feel this when he said, "For God has not given us a spirit of fear, but of power, love, and a sound mind." The more we put on our lion-like nature, the better it fits. And when the intimidator roars at us to make us fearful, we just roar back, and keep plundering his house.

I heard of an evangelist who was preaching a city-wide campaign in which there were many conversions occurring at his nightly meetings. Very late one night there was a knock at the door of the evangelist's hotel room. When he answered, there before him stood a visible emanation of Satan himself. The evangelist was a seasoned spiritual leader, and in his old-codger way simply said, "only you," and then he shut the door and went back to bed. That is how we handle the intimidator and his outlandish attempts to make us fearful. But you just cannot intimidate a lion—and we are lions!

For a couple of decades my primary calling was in youth ministry. One of the marvelous things about working with eleven- to eighteen-year-old students is that you see many of them take their first step of faith with Christ. In the back of my mind was this well-quoted statistic: "Ninety percent of the people who ever make a decision for Christ do so before the age of 20."[6] That motivated me. I (Jon) started an annual youth camp in the mid-1980s and it continued for more than twenty years. On a mountain in northeast Alabama I literally saw thousands of young people come to faith and give their lives to Christ. I share this because it was also a place of great spiritual warfare.

I would pray through most nights at the camp. I could feel the attack, the intimidation that Verlon detailed. Through prayer with the leadership team we prevailed as sons and daughters of almighty God. We experienced peace, salvation, deliverance, and victory that was a result of intentional frontlines prayer.

The Deceiver

If Satan's attempt to bring a dark cloud over us does not discourage us, and if his attempt to intimidate us does not thrust us into fear, he will likely move to the tactic of deception. In 2 Corinthians 11:14–15, Paul told the church not to be surprised when Satan disguises himself as an angel of light. Dating clear back to the garden of Eden, the devil deceived Eve by leading her to question the motives of God. Using slightly altered truths is Satan's game, and he is pretty good at it.

We see this shift in strategy in Nehemiah's story. After the threats and intimidation did not stop the builders on the wall, a man from one of the nearby towns showed up pretending to be a friend and told Nehemiah that an attack was coming right then, and he should run to a back room and hide. Actually, there was no attack coming; it was only a ploy to make Nehemiah look like a frail leader to weaken the resolve of the builders. Nehemiah's answer to that deceiver was brilliant; he said he was simply too busy on this important work to go hide. And with that, he turned to resume his supervision of his men.

Here is the big point: a strong sense of purpose and dogged commitment to one's mission naturally protects leaders from being vulnerable to the deceiver and his deceptions. King David's adulterous affair with Bathsheba would not have happened if he had been where he was supposed to be—on the battlefield "when kings go to war," rather than on the palace roof watching women bathe (see 2 Samuel 11:1–2). Balaam would not have found himself trying to bless an evil king if he had stuck to God's script rather than being so interested in a big paycheck (see Numbers 22). Sometimes it's the voice of logic, sometimes it's lust, and sometimes it's greed, but in all of these things the deceiver got the upper hand because people softened their unwavering commitment to their mission. In 2 Timothy 4:7, Paul spoke about his calling and his commitment in those famous words; "I have fought the good fight, I have finished the race, I have kept the faith." May we take a lesson from the likes of Paul and Nehemiah who stayed on task and simply stayed too busy with their calling to be affected by the deceiver.

Intimidation and deception are like a one-two punch. When we fall for them, we get sidelined. People can be a hindered through discouragement, feelings of unworthiness, and failure. The way we are overcomers against these attacks is by knowing who we are in Christ. Our position as believers gives us not just the advantage in the battle, but assures us of victory over darkness. We lean into knowing we are children belonging to God, heirs of the kingdom, a chosen nation, a holy race, and royal priesthood. We are given spiritual weapons that are mighty. Ultimately, there is nothing that can separate us from the love of God (see Romans 8:37–39). Living with this posture keeps us on the mission, strengthens our resolve, and encourages us from the inside out.

3

A SIMPLE THEOLOGY OF PRAYER

We are warmed by fire, not by the smoke of
the fire. We are carried over the sea by a ship,
not by the wake of a ship.

—THOMAS MERTON[1]

We realize that this chapter will make some people very nervous. Those in the body of Christ who hold a high view of God's sovereignty shudder to talk about any authority being given to Satan or man for reasons of deflating God's majesty! And this is a solid theological concern. However, I (Verlon) come from the portion of the body of Christ that holds a high view of God's empowerment of the saints for the advancement of the mission. That, too, is a solid theological position. Given this tension, I ask you to please be patient with us as we walk this theological tightrope and place the vocation of prayer in a different light.

Forty years ago, I had an interesting conversation with my father. He had been a pastor for many years and held his calling very seriously. I was a freshly minted ordained minister and serving in my first church. I don't remember the topic we were discussing, but it led to me saying, "Well, if it is God's will, it'll happen." My father was typically a quiet man, so I was surprised when he furrowed his brow and asked, "Son, where did you get a piece of theology like that?" While I fumbled around for a response on that day, I have reflected on his question dozens of times since. The truth is, I was too young in my Christian leadership maturity to fully appreciate the nature of the spiritual battle or appreciate our human capacity to move the hand of God through prayer. My dad's words have reverberated in my soul over the years and pushed me again and again to form a well-developed theology of prayer. Perhaps this chapter will do the same for you.

Why do you pray? Is it because Christians are supposed to? Is it because it helps you manage your stress? Is it because prayer aligns you to God's voice? Is it because your best ideas come to you when you have quieted yourself in prayer? Or maybe is it because you feel the need for fellowship with the Lord? While all of these are beneficial, they do not capture the most potent active ingredient of prayer.

The Prince of the Air

I approach this topic with caution, knowing full well how difficult it is for many to balance Satan's authority and God's sovereignty. But there is some theological work to be done here if our prayer lives are to become as potent as intended by our Lord.

Many scholars approach this topic by means of the "already/not yet" nature of the kingdom of God. In other words, many things have already been delivered to us as a result of Jesus' victory on the cross, while other things are victories still to come. Thus, due to the "not yet" reality, Satan still has an ability to affect things upon the earth. Many Christian songs and bumper stickers make it sound like God is actively directing all things at all times. Actually, that is not quite true. Since the fall of man, and man's decisions in the garden to ignore the counsel of God in favor of the counsel of the serpent, Satan became the prince and power of the air. Paul acknowledged this in Ephesians 2:2 when he said, "You once walked according to the course of this world, according to the prince of the power of the air." Notice the connection in Paul's words between the "course of this world" and the "prince of the power of the air." We must recognize that a measure of earthly authority has landed in our spiritual enemy's hands for this season.

The Old Testament reveals a picture of the interplay between humanity's prayer, divine response, and Satan's resistance in Daniel 9–10. Daniel had been in fasting and prayer for three weeks over the mournful condition of Jerusalem. On the twenty-fourth day as he was taking a walk along the banks of the Tigris River, he was visited by an angel. The angel reported to him heaven had heard his prayer three weeks back, but the prince over that realm resisted the angel that was sent to Daniel with the divine reply. But now, after the archangel Michael intervened, he was finally free to meet Daniel that day beside the river. Here we see that the prince of the air had the power to withhold an angel of God—at least for a while. But Daniel's persistence in prayer enabled God's intervention to finally come forth.

There was an interesting exchange between Satan and Jesus recorded in Luke 4:5–7, where the devil offered Jesus all of the kingdoms of the world if He would merely bow in worship to Satan. While we usually focus on Jesus' answers, it does us well to pause and realize a powerful undertone—Satan actually held the earthly kingdom in his hands to offer Jesus. And Jesus did not correct him about his domain. Later in Jesus' ministry, he again acknowledged Satan's authority over the earth when he sent his seventy-two disciples to go into the towns and preach the gospel. Though I mentioned this earlier, it is worth repeating that their success was obvious to Jesus in Luke 10:18 because He saw Satan actually falling from the sky. In other words, the disciples' work in healing, teaching about the kingdom of God, and casting out demons caused Satan to lose some of his positional authority over the earth as the prince and power of the air. While it is true that at the cross Satan was defeated, it is also true that the "not yet" nature of the kingdom of God means the strongman is still sowing his deeds of darkness in our world.

This, then, is the situation in which we find ourselves: though we have the kingdom of God ruling our hearts, families, and home, we still live in a world that is affected by the prince and power of the air. This, then, is why we pray—to invite the will and the plans of God onto the earth. As residents of the earth, we have the right to invite the Lord into our spaces as we desire. Though the temporary landlord of this earth will protest and resist our prayers for the interventions of God, we still have the right to choose the will of God to fill our lives, our families, our ministries, and our neighborhoods.

One pastor of a church in South Korea felt called to reach out to Japanese people. But when he held evangelistic crusades in Japan, he noted that the people's eyes glazed over as the gospel was proclaimed, and it made no sense to them. In response to those failures he decided to fly planeloads of Japanese people to South Korea. When they heard the gospel preached there, the words were clear, and many came to Christ easily. This pastor's explanation was that their prayer teams had prayed an opening over Seoul, and there existed a spiritual freedom that was not present in Japan. In other words, the prince and power of the air had less authority to suppress the gospel in the areas where consistent and bold prayer had been practiced. The Scriptures have called us to be a people of prayer, not because it is a spiritual thing to do, but because God waits for His people to call for His interventions to come to earth and push back the plans of the prince of the air.

The Authority of Man

For now, God allows the prince and power of the air to continue in his limited authority. However, God has others who hold great authority on the earth too: us. Interestingly, God tends to wait for us to exercise our authority in prayer before He intervenes. Never is this seen more clearly then in James 4:8: "Draw near to God and He will draw near to you." The first step toward God is ours to make. While I fully believe in the kind of grace that draws sinners to the Father even before they know Him (prevenient grace), there is still a divine pattern in place where the Father waits for His creation to make the first move. Jesus' story of the prodigal son emphasizes this divine restraint. In this story the father waits until he sees the figure of his son in the distance, then he runs to his son, embraces him, restores him, and plans an immediate celebration (see Luke 15:23). What a great picture of divine respect for the authority and autonomy of His creation. Revelation 3:20 reveals another picture of this where Jesus is knocking on the heart's door but not entering until it is opened up to Him.

This principle of the divine waiting upon the created is an important thing to understand about the necessity of prayer—the first move is ours to make. Jesus again made this point in Matthew 16:19: "Whatever you bind on earth will be bound in heaven, and whatever you loose on earth will be loosed in heaven." That is a powerful truth that few American Christians and churches have fully embraced. We have the authority to suppress the enemy's activity on earth, and we have the authority to release God's activity to flow upon earth. The early Celtics called these heaven-meets-earth occurrences "thin places." They would often greet each other with, "Hello brother, have you been to the 'thin place' lately?"[2] These thin places are locations and moments where the veil that separates the man-world from the God-world is so thin that one can peer into the activities of God and see what He is doing. Thin places are real, and we have been given the authority to help create them; the profound activity of ushering the kingdom of God into our homes, our neighborhoods, and our cities is in our hands. Heaven is waiting for us to make the first authoritative move in prayer and call for His kingdom to come.

What is it that will motivate us to make that first move? That is a real question. I love Eugene Peterson's answer: "Prayer is an act of defiance against the current regime."[3] There is no greater motivation to use our authority than in response to the current regime's mistreatment of our families and our neighbors. If you are not frustrated by the oppressions of the prince and power of the air, then your Christianity needs a serious reboot. Frustration over Satan's regime and dark advancements should inspire powerful prayers in the life of the church. And when we knock upon heaven's door, we should expect the kingdom to break forth in some way into our situations. We have been given such an authority for just such a reason.

When Jesus Regained the High Ground

The penitent process that had been set up by the law of Moses was designed to invite God into the affairs of men in response to righteousness. While this version of opening a door to the divine had been effective for seven hundred years, it left something to be desired. According to Paul in Galatians 3:24–25, the law had been a good tutor, but something more perfect was needed. So, the coming of Christ replaced the law of righteousness with faith in Christ Jesus. His incarnation instituted the day of salvation, and His resurrection demonstrated God's power over the prince of the air.

However, the greatest victory was not Jesus' victory over death; it was in what He did next. Jesus assumed His eternal role by taking the place at the right hand of the Father to advocate for us night and day. Jesus explained this role to His disciples before He left the earth in John 10:7, 9 where He repeated that He was the door between heaven and earth. Simply stated, by assuming His post-resurrection role as the continual door between heaven and earth, mankind now has immediate and certain access to the resources of heaven just for the asking. According to Matthew 7:7 we can now simply ask, and it will be given; seek and we will find; knock and it will be opened to us. Wow! We have the power to actually open a door between heaven and earth, because Jesus is that door. And by becoming the revolving door between the power of heaven and the affairs of earth, Jesus regained the high ground for the kingdom of God and assured that there would be much more divine activity flowing upon the earth in response to the prayers of His people.

The *Missio Dei*

The recent century has proved to be very rich for the church for many reasons, perhaps the greatest of which is the recovery of the apostolic theology of *sentness*. The recovery of this historic theology officially began in 1932 at the Brandenburg Missionary Conference in Berlin, when Karl Barth lectured on the *missio dei*—the mission of God.[4] While the *missio dei* was engaged in theological circles throughout the twentieth century, it got a serious lift by Princeton Theology Professor Darrel Guder in 2000, and his book *The Continuing Conversion of the Church*. The *missio dei* is best defined in John 20:21: "As the Father has sent Me, I also send you." Once one embraces the theology of *sentness,* it prompts the question: "Sent to do what?" For that answer we must look to why the Father sent the Son. According to 1 John 3:8, Jesus was sent to destroy the works of the devil. So then, we, too, are sent to destroy the plans of Satan by opening the door that ushers in the plans of God. To put it a different way, John 12:46 says we are "sent" to dispel the darkness by turning on the lights of God, just like Jesus did. It is the mission of the church to continue the mission of Christ—to plunder the house of the strongman and destroy his evil works. The deeper forms of prayer seriously embrace the dual vocations of ushering in the interventions of God and ruining the plans of the enemy to devour people on our watch.

Often as I (Jon) engage in the *missio dei,* I find myself praying in terms of light and darkness, because I know that sometimes there is a specific evil to be confronted. I pray on Tuesday mornings with some other pastors in our community. We will be moved to pray for certain issues from time to time: an election, our government, and our schools, for example. In doing so, we come against the darkness with the light of Christ; we pray fervently for darkness to be dispelled. We often pray against the social ills of addiction, pornography, and other traps Satan uses to rob, kill, and destroy mankind.

The Keys to the Kingdom

Given the theology that we are sent to help usher in the Father's will upon the earth, we need to have confidence in our authority to do so. We only have to again look to Jesus' words for this authorization: "And I will give you the keys of the kingdom of heaven, and whatever you bind on earth will be bound in heaven, and whatever you loose on earth will be loosed in heaven" (Matt. 16:19). Wow, that is a lot of authority!

The vast majority of Christians do not realize they have keys in their pocket that actually open doors in heaven. But that is exactly what Jesus gave to us. With us holding such keys, why don't we use them more often and with greater confidence? That is the question that is probably reverberating in the halls of heaven. I have to wonder if we could overhear a couple of angels talking, if it might sound something like this: "Why don't they open up the door between heaven and earth more often? Why don't they just download the Father's will when they get in trouble? Don't they realize they have the keys to the door that changes everything?" Whether or not those conversations occur, we have been given the keys to open the door whenever we feel the need. But do we see prayer as a key for an actual door? And do we know how to turn that key? That is precisely the definition of prayer—twisting the key in the door of heaven and watching God's interventions pour forth upon the earth. The prince of the air can only exercise his authority if we are not exercising our authority; he can only withhold God's plans so long as we are not insisting upon God's plans. But once we pull out our keys and open up heaven's doors, then God's will and God's interventions pour onto the earth unabated. And that is the simple theology of prayer.

4

INVITING THE KINGDOM
ONTO EARTH

My soul does not find itself unless it acts.

—THOMAS MERTON[1]

The essential first step to opening up heaven's doors is to acknowledge that we actually have the keys to those doors in our possession. It is easy to follow the common axiom, "Let go and let God." And as spiritual and faith-filled as it sounds to back off and let God run the universe, He has chosen to put the responsibility on us to call forth the kingdom of God onto the earth. Simply stated, if the interventions of God are going to show up on the earth, it is going to be because someone on earth asked for them. That is not an activity of letting go; rather, it's an activity of calling forth.

I (Jon) had the privilege and honor of planting a church that launched publicly in 2007. We started with six people in a Bible study in March of 2006. That grew to about twenty in six months. We were about to start

Sunday worship. We were still under the radar of the community—we were pretty much a group of people with me as their priest and a website. Given we had not started a Sunday service, we had this window of opportunity where we could do a church retreat on a full weekend. So, we went about an hour away to a conference center and my friend Steve Fry came to speak to seventeen people about being a church in Oviedo, Florida.

Steve came with a very profound word that got woven into our DNA. He called us to be an outpost for the kingdom of God in this world. The very land where we inhabited was to be like the kingdom and when people looked at this new little church, they would be able to glimpse the kingdom of God. What would they see? I intentionally chose not to have a mission or vision statement; instead, we would have a Rule of Life as a congregation. We did have measurable goals—benchmarks to propel us forward—but our mission was already defined. Our Rule of Life was anchored in the Great Commandment: "Love God with all you are and love one another" (see Matthew 22:36–40), and the Great Commission: "Therefore go and make disciples of all nations, baptizing them in the name of the Father and of the Son and of the Holy Spirit, and teaching them to obey everything I have commanded you" (Matt. 28:19–20 NIV).

We see the kingdom of God in this world when the church is loving God, loving each other, and loving the world with gospel:

The Great Commandment

+

The Great Commission

=

A Great Church Living the Kingdom Life

There was a First Commission given to humanity in Genesis 1:28: "And God said to them, 'Be fruitful and multiply and fill the earth and subdue it, and have dominion over the fish of the sea and over the birds of the heavens and over every living thing that moves on the earth.'" God's original intent is for humanity to rule the earth in covenant relationship with Him. The kingdom comes when we take seriously the First Commission and marry it to the Great Commission.

Kingdom Prayers Are Not Done Alone

Requesting the inbreaking kingdom of God to arrive upon the earth is not a small initiative, which is the reason the task has been given to the church and not individuals. Robert Mulholland pointed out that the first phrase in the Lord's Prayer is "Our Father," not "My Father." Such a weighty thing as prayer is difficult to practice as an individual.[2] This insight is regularly overlooked in individualistic cultures like America. In a collectivistic society like Jesus lived in, salvation and prayer were group events. Thus, the New Testament assumed that prayer would be offered by and pour upon the entire group and the entire nation. Only in individualistic societies can prayer be practiced in such a way that one could become more self-centered for having prayed. But this is not what the Lord had in mind when He taught on prayer. He assumed that the disciples would be engaging in this prayer together. In Matthew 26:38–41, when He was in Gethsemane and in deep personal distress, He twice asked the disciples to stay up and pray with Him. Even in His darkest personal valley, He desired that it be a corporate event.

Some of the great leaders during the Great Awakening recognized the calling of praying together. Jonathan Wesley referred to the need for social holiness, by which he meant that our spiritual growth requires the prayers and engagement of our brothers and sisters. Similarly, a story is told of D. L. Moody as he was visiting a prominent Chicago citizen when the idea of church membership and involvement came up. The man said, "I believe I can be just as good a Christian outside the church as I can be inside it." Moody said nothing. Instead, he moved to the fireplace, blazing against the winter outside, removed one burning coal, and placed it on the hearth. The two men sat together and watched the ember die out. Then the other man said, "I see."[3]

If this is true for our personal Christian formation, it is doubly true for the prayers needed to advance the kingdom mission. Calling for kingdom interventions are best practiced as corporate prayer activities. Robert Mulholland said, "Corporate spirituality will wither on the vine if it does not reach out into the world."[4] The

New Testament term *ekklesia* means "out" and "to call," which Robert Anderson interprets to mean that people are called out of their normal pursuits to carry a specific function, and that it is always used to address the assembly and never the people that compose that assembly.[5] The mission of praying in the interventions of God onto the earth is an activity for the whole body of Christ; it is a corporate endeavor.

This idea of corporate prayer is at the foundation in my tribe of Anglicanism. In the English Reformation, the *Book of Common Prayer* was crafted and people could now pray together in their own native tongue. As you already know, I find the *Book of Common Prayer* to be an amazing and rich resource for the prayer life of the church. The gathering of believers in corporate prayer binds us together as an expression of the kingdom of God on the earth.

The corporate prayer assumption is seen in Exodus 17:11–12 when the children of Israel faced the Amalekites in battle. Moses went up the hill and held the rod, signifying the authority of God over his head. Whenever he held the rod up, Israel began to prevail, and whenever he got tired and put down the rod to rest his arms, the Amalekites began to prevail. Finally, Aaron and Hur stood beside Moses, holding up his arms throughout the day until Israel overpowered their enemy and won the battle. Let's look honestly at this story: Israel only prevailed if Moses upheld the rod of God's authority, and yet it required human strength to keep the rod in the raised position. With the battle continuing throughout the heat of the day, Moses needed help keeping the intervention of God flowing for the troops. Could there be any clearer picture for the present-day church? We have the authority in our hands to call forth God's interventions upon the earth, but it will take a group effort in prayer to keep us all strengthened and encouraged until God's plans arrive and give victory.

We Are the Ones to Open the Doors to God's Plans

This is the cornerstone of prayer: that we are the ones who initiate God's plans upon the earth. Our Lord holds many great plans and interventions for all of the dark corners of our world, but He needs us to invite them in. In Ezekiel 22:30, we see God lamenting that He needed someone on earth to *stand in the gap* between God and earth, but He could find no one. The point? God's plan does not show up in our world effectively until there is someone to call for it. In a paradoxical twist, the limitless God waits for limited men and women to usher in His interventions; God's plans are up to us to initiate. And this "stand in the gap" theology did not dissipate with the coming of Jesus as some have presumed. This was why Jesus instructed His disciples in Matthew 6:10 that their first prayer should be calling on the will of God to be done on earth as it is done in heaven. We invite the Lord's inbreaking kingdom or the inbreaking does not occur in its fullness. We can always hope someone else in the body of Christ is actively inviting the Lord's interventions, but it is assigned to all of us to call on plans of the

Lord to pour forth into the darkness that is at work all around us.

Everyone has a different view and sees different forms of darkness at work around them, so everyone needs to pray for the Lord's interventions into their lives, their neighborhoods, and their ministries. Truthfully, it does not take a spiritual giant to see the darkness at work around us. When I walk around just one city block in Seattle, I can easily see the strongman's kingdom plans for my neighbors and neighborhoods. Watching the drug deals on the corners, the runaway teen crouched against a bus enclosure, and drunken people ambling down the sidewalk in daylight hours reveals that Satan's kingdom is holding a noticeable upper hand in my town. This is probably true in your city, too, and should be a great disturbance in the souls of the Christians who live there. This is the stuff that has historically motivated God's people to arise in powerful prayer through the ages. The American church has some ground to make up to see God's plans become more visible on our streets than the strongman's plans.

In Matthew 16:18–19, Jesus gave His divine strategy to bring the day of salvation upon the earth. First, He used common people like Peter and you and me to build His church. Second, He decided to give the keys to the doors of heaven to His followers. And, third, He promised that divine interventions would pour out of those doors whenever His people opened them in prayer. That was and is Christ's singular strategy to flood the earth with the kingdom of God and contend for the souls of men and women. Obviously, our role is to use our keys that He left with us and open those doors. Pastor and author Dan Kimball noted from John 17:15–18 that Jesus did not want us to create a Christian subculture, but rather He prayed that we remain in the world to redeem the world.[6] Believers who are immersed in Christian subcultures are probably not the ones who are using their keys to open heaven's doors; they are probably using their prayers to edify themselves, their families, and their church friends. May there be a revival of God's people who know that they have divine keys to open big doors for the kingdom, and they know how to use them.

There is another subtle but powerful point in the verse where Jesus gave us the authority to open heaven's door—He used the word "keys" rather than "key."[7] What this suggests is there are numerous kinds of prayers that open numerous doors. Some people muddle the potency of this verse by suggesting, "Prayer is the key." I do not see it that way. There are all kinds of prayers that open big doors in heaven, and there are all kinds of prayer keys that open these doors. Such keys are powerful when they are in the hands of those who are working on the white-hot, bleeding-edge, frontlines of the gospel.

When we pray, we are using the keys to call forth God's inbreaking kingdom upon the earth. This was very clear to the early church and is evidenced by the way prayer was so interspersed throughout their activities in the book of Acts. They knew the keys; they held the keys; they used the keys. We, too, must use our keys and learn to pray in powerful ways that befits our authority.

Remember, God's will does not flow upon the earth when He calls for it; His interventions flow when we call for it. We become soldiers on a mission, the means of grace for the hope of glory; we participate with God by praying prayers as the Holy Spirit leads.

Submission to God's Plans

If we are going to open up the doors of heaven and let kingdom plans come our way, we must be ready to accept the plans that pour forth. Even though we are called to use our keys and open heaven's door, we are not in charge of creating the kingdom plans that come out—our Father is. Thus, there is a necessary submission needed for anyone who uses his or her keys in prayer. If we become practiced at opening the door for the kingdom of God, we must be ready to accept the intervention and the timing of the intervention that come out.

There are numerous pictures in Scripture of the umbilical bond between prayer and submission. One notable example is in 2 Samuel 12:20 when David fasted and prayed for his and Bathsheba's baby who was very ill. After seven days of this prayer vigil, the child died. And, surprisingly, David washed his face, went to the house of the Lord to worship, and went home to eat dinner. His servants were confused because he shifted from grief to acceptance so fast. But they did not understand that David was a man after God's own heart and understood the necessary balance between compelling God for an answer and submitting to God's decision.

However, the greatest example of the relationship between prayer and submission is in Matthew 26:39 where Jesus asked the Father to let the cup of crucifixion pass from Him. Yet by the end of His prayer He submitted with the words, "Nevertheless, not as I will, but as you will." Jesus desired to open a door where relief might come forth, but the plan that came forth confirmed His death on a Roman cross. His surrender should be an example to all of us that we can pray for certain outcomes to flow from heaven, but it is our Christian heritage to accept the answers that actually flow forth. I have a personal theory that those who struggle to surrender to God's plans also struggle to use their keys to open heaven's doors. But those who are willing to accept whatever answers might flow forth are more likely to pull out their keys and boldly open big doors in prayer.

Author and Christian leader Charles Colson reveals a deep submission seen in the life of Dietrich Bonhoeffer, who at the time of his execution said a short prayer, then climbed the steps to the gallows in a calm and composed manner. A doctor who watched the event reported that in almost fifty years of working in the medical profession, he had never seen a man die so entirely submissive to the will of God.[8]

Bold prayer and deep submission have an unbreakable bond; bold prayers that are not rooted in submission are simply exercises of carnal desires. When Peter made this mistake in Matthew 16:23, Jesus said, "Get behind Me, Satan! . . . for you are not mindful of the things of God, but the things of men." We must be submitted to the things of God in order to pray for the interventions of God—whatever they might be.

Calling on the Provider

Every servant of the gospel has to learn to lean into the very nature of God as they pray. Our Lord's divine roles such as the Protector, Healer, Friend, and Redeemer cannot be separated from who He is when He is listening to our calls for action. This is also true when leaning into the Provider. Jesus recognized the Father as the Provider of all who live on the earth in Matthew 6:25–33, where He noted that the grass in the field, the birds in the air, and the people who roam the earth are all provided for. Jesus admonished us to relax in God's provision as a natural expectation of living on this earth. Perhaps this explains Jesus' approach to feeding the five thousand recorded in Matthew 14:19. We tend to focus on the multiplication miracle and almost miss Jesus' prayer where He looked up to heaven and, in so doing, called on His Father, the Provider, to feed the hungry crowd.

However, God's provisions can be slowed and challenged by the prince of the air. Every day our enemy is set on destroying us; he comes to rob, kill, and destroy (see John 10:10). Too often Christians are living as though they have no adversary. They live as though life is a tea party. Unfortunately, churches who aren't effective on the frontlines of evangelism drift into a comfort-based Christianity, and their people forget the calling to rush into the war zone for the sake of the lost. But for those who live on the frontlines, they see the struggle between God's inbreaking kingdom and the strongman's kingdom, and they feel the need to pull in prayer for God's plans to break forth.

We (Verlon) lived this reality in our Seattle story after our childcare was forced to close amidst legal action. This closure followed a year when our autism school director had contracted cancer, which had subsequently affected the school's enrollment and income. In total, these back-to-back losses had resulted in the loss of tens of thousands of dollars in monthly tuition, and several of our dinner churches that were funded by this income were now in distress. Suddenly the lightbulb went on in my head—defunding our efforts was the enemy's strategy against us. The strongman's plans to keep us from spreading dinner churches throughout our city like they did in Acts 5:28 was to frustrate our finances. And, even more sobering, his plans were being worked against us unabated—without any prayer resistance from us. When this truth sank in, a holy anger erupted from our church; a new boldness in prayer boiled up in us. The knowledge that the enemy had direct plans to drain our finances changed us. And that was the season when our ability to pull out our keys and open heaven's doors on behalf of our ministry calling became bold and unrelenting.

God is sovereign and His will cannot be thwarted forever. He is Lord and King. He is the Christus Victor! Yet with victory ultimately secured, we are still in a battle. There will still be constant attacks on our finances, our health, our communities of faith, and our neighborhoods. So, we pray bold prayers of taking authority and dominion.

The Constant Flow

Beyond the role of Provider, our Lord serves the roles of Protector, Healer, Teacher, Redeemer, and Encourager—just to name a few. What this means when we open up heaven's doors in prayer is that we are talking to the one who cannot help Himself from being Himself and flowing out to the need once the doors are open to Him.

Saint Teresa of Avila, the fifteenth-century contemplative, taught that God's grace was like streams that are constantly flowing down upon the earth to refresh us.[9] Knowing God's natural propensity toward us means that our prayers are more about directing God's favor than inspiring God's favor. Many Christians approach prayer like they are needing to pry answers out of a stingy heaven, when, in fact, they are opening up doors that God is hungry to open, and directing healing, protection, provision, teaching, encouragement, and many other divine graces to points of need that we see upon this earth.

We are all under spiritual attack every day. We might not realize it, but the devil is always after us. It is most often through temptation that the enemy pursues us. All of us have recently heard of noble Christian leaders who have fallen into sin, destroyed their leadership, lost their families, and disturbed the faith of their congregations who trusted and respected them. I have watched friends make horrible sinful decisions that destroyed everything they had. A dear friend was in this situation a few years after the 9/11 attacks and was sent to me for counsel. He was trying to dismiss, justify, and downplay his actions and I remember telling him, "Your home is ground zero and like the evil that took those buildings down, you flew jets into your home and community." The destructive power of sin is real and devastating, which is why we stand firm against the fiery darts of the devil with the whole armor of God.

I was given charge of a retreat center that was in a difficult season. It was failing and, in reality, hanging by a thread, about to close its doors. It was a wonderful place, a forty-eight-acre oasis in a suburb of Orlando. However, I learned that it was compromised spiritually. A lot of darkness had come on the campus. Groups had been welcomed on the campus that had beliefs and practices that were antithetical to the gospel of Jesus; one such group that came often would have seances in the chapel. When we discovered this, we began to pray and to discern there were dark strongholds at the center.

I would distinguish the difference between daily spiritual warfare and strongholds.

It was a different and more direct kind of warfare; there were things of spiritual darkness operating on the property. In a spiritual sense, they had been given permission to be there almost as if they had a deed to the territory. When we realized this, we took on a different posture of prayer from 2 Corinthians 10:3–6:

For though we live in the world, we do not wage war as the world does. The weapons we fight with are not the weapons of the world. On the contrary, they have divine power to demolish strongholds. We demolish arguments and every pretension that sets itself up against the knowledge of God, and we take captive every thought to make it obedient to Christ. And we will be ready to punish every act of disobedience, once your obedience is complete. (NIV)

Our prayers had to take on an aggressive destructive stance. We began doing prayer walks around the property. The staff, our board, and our friends began to pray against the strongholds, demolishing them with the mighty weapons in our arsenal given to us by almighty God. It wasn't all at once, but slowly we dismantled the strongholds brick by brick. It was like a cloud lifted and once again light shined on this refuge and we saw the center redeemed by God, becoming a sacred space of His dwelling, where people could encounter Him every day.

Paul's text speaks to another issue. We live in an age where, at least in the public arena, truth is getting harder to discern. There are agenda-driven politics and if there is disagreement, then it is war. There is rampant injustice being justified, endorsed, and, even in some places, blessed. As we in the cultural West delve deeper into a post-Christendom mindset, we live in a society that has abandoned a commonsense idea of what is right and wrong. We live with relativism and subjectivism, everyone doing what is right in their own mind. Pastor Tony Evans once famously said, "Jesus did not come to take sides; He came to take over!"[10]

There is a call to align ourselves fully with God and His ways. A relativism and subjectivism has creeped into our seminaries and churches, into leadership and whole denominations. Paul warned of this in 2 Corinthians 10:5, encouraging the church that, "We demolish arguments and every pretension that sets itself up against the knowledge of God, and we take captive every thought to make it obedient to Christ."

We may not agree on economic strategies, foreign policy, or even moral issues facing our day. There are merits to a variety of positions that are taken. Can we care and provide for the refugees, the poor, and the needy while at the same time protect our national borders? Can we care for the least of these while defending the nation against aggression? I do believe the way to bring about a civil unity is to submit ourselves to Christ, to be on His side, taking every thought captive to Him and then being loving, kind, generous, and compassionate, as He is.

We must realize that some of the tensions we find ourselves in are on a level of spiritual warfare, frontline prayer. Let us recognize this and pray for a supernatural, God-inspired, and anointed unity to descend and for the Prince of Peace to reign. There is a constant flow of grace ready to flood out of heaven, and our prayers direct that abounding favor toward the pain and darkness that is oppressing those around us. One of Teresa of Avila's famous statements is: "Christ has no body on earth but yours, no hands but yours."[11] Her point is not lost: it is up to us to steer God's grace in its many forms toward the earth. There is no one else here but us; the keys to heaven's doors have been left in our hands.

5

FOCUSED ON THE FAMILY RESCUE BUSINESS

Happiness consists in finding out precisely what the "one thing necessary" may be, in our lives, and in gladly relinquishing all the rest. . . . Each one of us is called to a special place in the Kingdom.

—THOMAS MERTON[1]

One of the earliest heartbeats that servants on the front-lines of evangelism need is the pulsating knowledge that they are called to directly engage in the divine priority—the rescue of the lost. This level of prayer assumes that one knows they are not only saved, but they are also sent into the mission of Christ. Until a person feels called to this deeper level of their salvation, focusing their prayers on the rescue of others will seem weighty and overbearing. However, each of us is called to take our place in the God-family rescue business; this family concern is our first prayer concern.

The God-Family Business

There is little doubt what business the God-family is engaged in. Jesus made this clear in Luke 4, when He read from the scroll of Isaiah at the beginning of His ministry:

> "The Spirit of the LORD is upon Me,
> Because He has anointed Me
> To preach the gospel to the poor;
> He has sent Me to heal the brokenhearted,
> To proclaim liberty to the captives
> And recovery of sight to the blind,
> To set at liberty those who are oppressed;
> To proclaim the acceptable year of the Lord."
>   (vv. 18–19)

He then rolled up the scroll and said, "Today this Scripture is fulfilled in your hearing" (v. 21). This was not only His personal mission statement, but was revelatory of the family business. Then, in Luke 19:10, He stated it even more directly: "For the Son of Man came to seek and save those who are lost" (NLT). Every frontlines servant must hear this priority loudly: the God-family is in the rescue business.

The early apostles heard it and started referring to Jesus as the Savior of the world, which is the same thing as calling him the Rescuer of the world. Even further, the apostle Paul started using an interesting phrase in 2 Corinthians 6:2: "now is the day of salvation." By this he was naming the season in human history from the time of Christ till the present, in which ingathering of the lost is the overarching order of the day. There is coming a day when the season of ingathering will be over, but for now it continues. In fact, you and I are living in the gasping final moments of the day of salvation. Christianity is the greatest rescue project in the history of the world. This rescue priority is where the triune God is applying their greatest passion, and this rescue season is the time in which they are pursuing their greatest ingathering.

Sent

While this topic will be looked at again in a later chapter, it is important that we find our place in the rescue initiative that our Lord is focused upon. In Isaiah 6:8, we see a divine encounter that changed the trajectory of Isaiah's life and ministry. He experienced a vision in which he was taken to the throne room of God. Upon arrival, he felt unworthy to be in the presence of God in this way. Then an angel touched him and purged his sin. But what interests me most is what happened next, because God said to everyone in the room: "Whom shall we send?" Of course, the story ends with Isaiah blurting out that he was willing to be sent, but God's question is a haunting one that deserves some deep meditation on the part of every Christian. Those who get close to God will hear Him saying things like: "Whom can we send? Who will go? Who will engage in our rescue endeavors upon the earth?" And those who feel His heartbeat say, "Here am I, send me!" Do you know what God is talking about most in His courtroom? Sentness! And do you know why? Because He needs us to do our part in the kingdom rescue business!

Mission Drift

The American church is suffering today. Only 15 percent of churches across all denominational lines are growing, and only 1 percent is growing from evangelism.[2] The family rescue business has become negatively affected by surface pursuits and has all but lost its ability to rescue lost people. Author David Benner notes that clear back in 1905 the focus of the church shifted from the "cure of souls" to "pastoral counseling," and from "saving souls" to "supporting self-realization."[3] These dilutions have grown for the simple reason that it is an easier and more professional pastoral assignment than rescuing the lost. And here is where we find ourselves one hundred years later—we are doing almost everything in our churches except reaching the lost.

Jesus is still in the rescue business, but statistically most of His churches in the United States are not. They do not know how to rescue people who have been raised with a secular worldview, and they do not know how to pray effective rescue-focused prayers. What is considered a normal prayer life in many American churches is far afield from the kinds of prayers that would align with the greatest rescue project in the history of the world. Today many content themselves to pray outlines like the mnemonic device A-C-T-S: Adoration, Confession, Thanksgiving, and Supplication.[4] While these prayers are helpful to edify the saint, they do little to rescue the neighboring sinner. John Ortberg points out that Jesus was perfectly capable of laying out five principles for dynamic prayer; the fact that He didn't do it should make us pause and reflect.[5] Our inability to pray powerful prayers for the lost coupled with our inability to rescue the lost are the dual reasons for our wide-scape mission drift.

The Rescue-Focused Prayer

All forms of prayer are not equal; some prayers are more important than others. Jesus left behind the ninety-nine and pursued the one. This teaches us that rescuing the perishing is of a higher priority than comforting the found. So, praying bold prayers for the sinner is of a higher priority than praying edify-me prayers for the already saved. Let me hasten to say, I pray all kinds of edification prayers for my family, my church, and myself. However, there is a prayer-form that is simply of greater priority than personal edification. As noted in chapter 1, Jesus taught His disciples to start their prayers with "Thy kingdom come" before praying "give us this day our daily bread." Even Paul listed different forms of prayer in Ephesians 6:18–19, but clearly prioritized the bold prayers that would "make known the mystery of the gospel." There is great need today to reevaluate and re-win the practice of the rescue-focused prayer.

Not everyone ignores evangelism prayers. However, many evangelism prayers that are offered are simply too broad to be poignant. We live in a day where secular worldviews have separated from Christian worldviews to the point that a great chasm exists between the two. Broad evangelism strategies and in-kind prayer efforts are often shotgun approaches that can have a positive effect, but are not always the most effective. With the secular culture distancing themselves to the degree we are seeing today, we also need a rifle-like targeted missiology that can reach them. The large citywide campaigns worked better fifty years ago. Today, the strategies that focus on a particular people group and figures out how to do church with them are the kind of evangelism that is effective. Similarly, the prayers that are focused on particular people groups and neighborhoods and pray for people by name are the prayer-forms that pair well with the evangelism that is gaining traction today. Tom Clegg proposes that we make friends with sinners and then pray as if our friend's life depends on it, because it does.[6] The kingdom advances when rescue-focused prayers are burning hot in the hearts of Christ's people, and when they are contending for the souls of their neighbors whom they know by name.

A Burden for the Lost

In the '50s and '60s, churches used the evangelist's model across America to bring the unsaved to Christ. The way it worked was that an evangelist was called who started nightly meetings to preach nothing but salvation sermons. At first there might be no sinners in the house, so the Christians would come to the altars at the end to pray for their unsaved friends and family to come to Christ—they were praying evangelism prayers. Soon their hearts would get hot with that prayer and a burden for the lost would settle on them. Night after night they would weep and travail before the Lord for the salvation of others. That travail would soon turn into action, and they would start inviting unsaved friends to these nightly meetings. God's Spirit would then compel the sinner until they made their way to Christ.

In my (Verlon's) father's church in the 1960s, they relied on evangelists to do the work of evangelism like so many others. Once they reached thirty-five conversions, he would shut down the evangelism meetings, because he felt that was the number his church could effectively disciple into maturity. For the next six months the whole church focused on fathering and mothering these new converts by taking them to Bible studies, fellowship gatherings, prayer meetings, discipleship events, and into their homes to eat and talk about Jesus. Then, after six months, my father would call a new evangelist and do it all over again. That was their redemption strategy—to grow by seventy conversions per year. Notice how evangelism prayer was the initial congregational activity of this redemption strategy; how a burden of prayer would descend upon the people; how they actually prayed on a burden for their lost friends.

While this is an evangelism strategy from a bygone era, it forwards the question: When do we focus on our lost acquaintances long enough for a burden of prayer to descend upon us? A burden for the lost and rescue-focused prayers will start to burn hot in our hearts—if we give those fires a chance to burn.

6

WILLING TO WAIT
UPON GOD

There must be a time . . . when the man who
makes plans forgets his plans, and acts as if
he had no plans at all.

—THOMAS MERTON[1]

Another important prayer key that has been given to the
church is being willing to wait upon the Lord for His
answers to develop. Elijah understood this principle of
prayer when he sat on the hill and asked God to end Israel's
drought, recorded in 1 Kings 18:42–44. He kept sending
his servant to see if any clouds were forming, and six times
the servant returned to report there was nothing but blue
skies. But on the seventh time, the servant reported that
a small cloud was starting to form, and soon the sky was
blackened with clouds that poured out a torrent of rain
before the day was done. But note that Elijah lingered in
prayer until the rain clouds started to form; he realized, in
the Spirit, that this was a waiting event.

Waiting

Waiting with the Lord is important to Him. Gordon Fee once said that a prayer-less life is one of practical atheism.[2] Conversely, the person who is willing to engage in more costly forms of prayer, like waiting upon the Lord, is a person who becomes strong in their faith and contributes to the growth of the kingdom in strong ways. And if our strength is not great when we begin, it will surely increase while we wait upon the Lord. David counseled us in Psalm 27:14: "Wait on the LORD, and He will strengthen your heart; wait I say, on the LORD." Isaiah 40:31 also pointed to this by saying, "Those who wait on the LORD shall renew their strength, they shall run and not be weary, and they shall walk and not faint." These verses make it clear that the mere act of waiting with the Lord strengthens us and empowers our resolve as we pray. Further, when we wait with the Lord, our human perspectives and God's perspectives start to sync; the man calculator and the God calculator start to add up the same; the man prayer and the God answer starts to align. In other words, during seasons of waiting, God is preparing to answer our prayers and we are preparing to answer His; in waiting, we are listening to each other.

The church must learn to wait on the Lord. His timing is always right. Jesus practiced a holy patience. In Mark 9 there is an account of a child possessed by a demon. The disciples were unable to free this child from the darkness. Jesus intervenes and the child is delivered and made whole. The story ends with this exchange:

"And when he had entered the house, his disciples asked him privately, 'Why could we not cast it out?' And he said to them, 'This kind cannot be driven out by anything but prayer'" (vv. 28–29 ESV). We must be faithful in prayer and trust for God to work in us and through us in His perfect time.

Some spiritual answers take time and cost time; they are simply too wonderful to blow in quickly. Just like a father might speak patience into his young child to sit and wait for a beautiful sunset, so the Lord calls us to wait for His beautiful answer to form. Waiting with the Lord restores our appreciation for how truly good He is at His job of running the universe and restores our confidence that He is readying Himself to pour out of heaven on our behalf. Often, His answers are just too wonderful for us to be anything but fully attentive when they come through that door headed earthward.

My (Verlon's) father was a man who believed in using this form of prayer. Often when I woke up in the mornings, I would find my father in the living room, wrapped in a blanket, waiting upon God. His Bible would be open on a chair, his eyes would be moist from tears, and the lights would be turned low. It was obvious that he had been there for many hours in those early mornings. Beyond that, he loved reading the biographies of Praying Hyde, George Mueller, and Earnest Plymire—all men of faith who waited on God until answers came forth. And he got me reading these men too. As a teen I was mesmerized by their stories of running out of money for food for their orphanages, and rather than sending out letters for support, they closed themselves in with God until food was delivered for a house full of children. I will forever be grateful to my father for imputing into my spirit the vision of wrapping in a blanket and waiting upon the Lord *until* answers were delivered. Now as I look back over my life, the greatest breakthroughs and the deepest answers that I have ever received from God came as I waited with Him. My father's prayer key, as old-fashioned as it seems, still works.

There are so many wonderful stories of waiting. I (Jon) think of the account of Simeon and Anna in Luke 2:22–40 in what is referred to as the Presentation of the Lord in the Jerusalem Temple. Simeon was given a promise that he would not die until he saw the Lord's Messiah. Simeon was filled with the Holy Spirit and waited, not minutes, days, months, or even years, but decades to see this promise fulfilled. This waiting breathes of hope and anticipation. Anna, an octogenarian, lived a relatively uneventful life. She basically lived in the temple in prayer and worship. Her gaze fixed on one thing: God's salvation and redemption, now manifested in this child. Simeon and Anna waited.

We don't like to wait. We want it—and we want it now! We live in an on-demand world of immediate gratification full of short tracks and shortcuts, fast food, and same-day Amazon delivery. We rush to the next thing. Yet Psalm 46 bids us to "Be still, and know that I am God" (v. 10). I believe the opposite of that is also true—if we are not still, we know not God. In other words, we miss Him. Just as Verlon described his father, we must realize waiting is not a passive act. We wait actively, immersed in prayer, God's Word, worshiping, and listening with all our senses.

A rarely referenced Old Testament scripture from the prophet Habakkuk reveals a wonderful posture of waiting:

> I will stand at my watch and station myself on the ramparts; I will look to see what he will say to me, and what answer I am to give to this complaint.
>
> Then the Lord replied: "Write down the revelation and make it plain on tablets so that a herald may run with it. For the revelation awaits an appointed time; it speaks of the end and will not prove false. Though it lingers, wait for it; it will certainly come and will not delay." (2:1–3 NIV)

We have to realize that God's timing may not be our timing, but He is never late. We are in need of developing a holy patience as we seek the frontline mission of seeing redemption and salvation manifest in this world. Yes, there is an urgency and the lethargy of the church must be activated, but we do so in God's timing. It is His mission to be fulfilled, so we stand ready, waiting.

Weep in the Heat

Spiritual harvests require us to endure the heat of the day. This is the spiritual order of things that is revealed in Psalm 126:5–6: "Those who sow in tears shall reap in joy. He who continually goes forth weeping, bearing seed for sowing, shall doubtless come again with rejoicing, bringing his sheaves with him." When we learn to weep in the heat, we see a harvest come forth one day. God values human tears; the ancients well understood this. Second Chronicles 34:27 reveals that the Lord heard them because they wept. In Jeremiah 13:17, we witness the prophet weeping in a secret place. And, again, in Lamentations 1:16, Jeremiah talked about weeping until his eyes ran down like water because the enemy had prevailed.

However, my (Verlon's) favorite Old Testament weeping hero was Nehemiah. The central theme of this book proposes that church leaders need to be effective with both the trowel and the sword, which is a metaphor borrowed from Nehemiah's strategy. Yet, Nehemiah's victory did not start off with a building or warring strategy—it started with tears. Nehemiah 1:3–4 records that when he heard about Jerusalem, he was in great distress that the wall around the city had been torn down, and that the gates had been burned. Upon hearing the news, he sat down and wept. And it was not just an evening of grief, it lasted for many days. Soon his tears turned into fasting, his fasting into prayer, his prayer into a desire for action, and, ultimately, into a strategy that was worth revealing to the king. But it began with tears! Truthfully, many of the victory stories in the Bible include someone at some point engaging in weeping prayer.

Jesus understood the weeping prayer. In Luke 6:21, He taught the value of tears during His Sermon on the

Mount: "God blesses you who weep now, for in due time you will laugh" (NLT). Another powerful usage of Jesus' weeping prayer was when He visited Martha and Mary after Lazarus's death. Their brother was dead. These two sisters were in deep grief and were facing an uncertain future. Jesus purposefully delayed in coming to visit them for the stated purpose of demonstrating the power of God. But when He saw the sisters, John 11:35 simply recorded: "Jesus wept." Jesus loved Martha and Mary because of the time He had spent with them, and so I am quite sure He felt moved by their grief. Jesus, more than any other figure in human history, practiced a divine empathy. He could enter a situation and feel the pain, the fear, the questions people had and, by His comforting presence, situations changed. He felt their grief and sorrow, so He wept. And yet, what if Jesus' tears were more than compassion?

I (Verlon) have a sense that He was not only moved to compassion but was moved to intercession while standing in the midst of the sisters. Once the theology of weeping prayer is understood, it is difficult to imagine Jesus not employing it for a request as great as this. Jesus' tears were central in the most powerful miracle in the New Testament to that point—raising Lazarus from the dead.

The New Testament writers recognized the place of tears in the work of God, but perhaps none more than what we see in selections from James 4:7–10: "Resist the devil and he will flee from you. Draw near to God and He will draw near to you. . . . Lament and mourn and weep! . . . and He will lift you up." These verses make it obvious that weeping prayer is necessary at times; it is a form of spiritual warfare. Martin Luther cried out, "My people are humiliated," and Mother Teresa cried out, "My people are hungry."[3] Most Christian leaders could learn from those who've learned to weep over the people they are sent to serve. After reading about Martin Luther and Mother Teresa, I found a tearful prayer emerging from my soul that sounded like this: "My people are invisible." This is the condition of many of the people that fill our dinner church rooms in Seattle and across the country. They are ignored and invisible. Their isolation breaks my heart and I find myself weeping in prayer for them.

The act of weeping in prayer is one of great honesty; it acknowledges the depth of human pain and the desperate need for God's intervention. Perhaps this is why weeping in prayer is so important because it signifies that we are fully immersed in the pain of the problem while at the same time fully insistent that God respond. The weeping prayer, perhaps more than any other form of prayer, positions the person praying as a bridge between human pain and heaven's power. It is a great way an intercessor can stand in the gap for others.

Becoming one who can fully engage in weeping prayer is not a comfortable endeavor, but it does open some doors in heaven that other forms of prayer will not. Thus, it is worth the struggle to have our soul shaped by tears. James White explains it this way: "We are first torn loose from earthly attachments and ambitions and then quickened to a divine concern for the world. He plucks the world out of our hearts . . . and then He hurls the world into our hearts."[4] It is the divine activity of tearing and the hurling that makes this prayer formation uncomfortable. And yet, if one wants to be powerful in moving the hand of God, they should expect the seasons of adversity to develop that prayer life. This developmental principle is probably most true when learning to use the key of weeping prayer.

Groanings

Groaning in prayer is another powerful key, though it is an assault to many people's sensibilities. Yet, we see this in Scripture too many times to ignore. This was certainly the case in 1 Samuel 1:9–20 with Hannah who was childless and in the temple groaning in such a way as to catch the eye of Eli the priest. When he realized she was not drunk, but was groaning in deep intercession, he felt a word from the Lord that she would have what she was requesting. And one year later, that was exactly what happened when Samuel was born. We cannot escape the truth that her groanings brought an answer from heaven. John 11:38 reports that the disciples heard Jesus groaning again to Himself as He walked to the tomb. But notice the word *again*; this was not the first time the disciples heard Jesus groaning in prayer, nor would it be the last. In Romans 8:26 we see groaning prayer again when Paul stated: "We do not know what we should pray, but the Spirit himself makes intercession for us with groanings which cannot be uttered." Make no mistake; groaning in prayer is one of the powerful keys that has been given to the church.

Travailing Prayer

There are times when heaven simply needs long seasons of sober prayer before a divine response is sent. While I certainly do not know all the reasons for this, it appears that there is such a thing as praying the price. I hate to appear mechanical on this point, but some needs require more prayer hours than others. These are the times when experienced intercessors pull out the key of travailing prayer. Daniel's story that was talked about earlier in Daniel 9–10 reveals an answer coming after twenty-four days of travailing prayer. In Luke 18:1–7, Jesus tells a parable about a widow who kept coming to the judge asking for justice in her situation. Finally, the judge became worn down by her persistence and agreed to hear her case and decide in her favor. After telling this story, Jesus directed His followers to be like that widow, to be persistent in prayer, to be determined, to not lose heart, and to cry out day and night until justice comes. This is what travailing prayer looks like. Again, in Ephesians 6:18, Paul instructed the church to "stay alert and be persistent in your prayers" (ESV). There are times when the Lord needs travailing and prevailing prayers from us to open the door of heaven equal to the need on earth.

While much about travailing prayer and praying the price is held in the mystery of God, there is a scriptural association between travail and childbirth—as if the one praying is tasked with birthing an answer onto the earth. Micah 4:10 is one such example when the prophet instructed the people of Zion to be in pain, like a woman in labor, and in time the Lord would deliver them. Notice with me that there is such a thing as "due time" when God's answers come forth. I like the due-time verses found in the New Testament too. Romans 5:6 says that "when we were without strength, in *due time* Christ died for the ungodly" (emphasis added). First Timothy 2:6 states that Christ "gave Himself a ransom for all, to be testified in *due time*" (emphasis added). And then 1 Peter 5:6 reveals the necessity of "humbl[ing] yourselves under the mighty hand of God, that He may exalt you in *due time*" (emphasis added). Simply put, travailing prayer is needed because there is a "due time" inherent in some of heaven's answers. And until the due time arrives, God needs His praying people to put their foot in the door and hold it open. If we dare to travail and birth divine answers upon the earth, we will have due-time answers of our own. In due time, a chronic challenge will dissipate; in due time, a new effectiveness will be delivered to a ministry; in due time, lost people will be rescued.

Prayer is comprehensive and engages us on every level—weeping, groaning, and travailing as Verlon describes. Prayer is more than words; it is an investment of all I am—body, soul, mind, and spirit. Prayer is physical. At priestly ordinations in my tribe, the candidate will often lie facedown before the bishop and fellow presbyters humbly receiving this call and vocation. I have been driven to my knees many times in prayer, as well as rejoicing. These external postures of prayer need to be connected to the soul and mind, our hearts and heads. In Colossians 3:1–2 we are told: "If then you have been raised with Christ, seek the things that are above, where Christ is, seated at the right hand of God. Set your minds and hearts on things that are above, not on things that are on earth."

After a season of this kind of prayer I (Jon) felt a call to go and work with young people in a certain church. It pressed on me and I believed the Lord in a real sense required me to step out in faith, so I did. I was a candidate for the open youth ministry position, but nothing had been promised. I loaded up my car and moved to this community, thinking I would find some gainful employment and work with the young people whether they hired me or not. After a few weeks, I freaked out. I had left a life—my family and friends—and my thoughts and feelings were running amuck. I thought I needed to go home and began to think about packing my bags. I paused and read through Philippians (kind of comfort-food Scripture to me), and as I came to this text, I knew I was done as I received what I needed. My situation did not make sense. It wasn't logical and there were all kinds of feelings swirling around my circumstance. After reading these verses, I cried out to God with weeping, deep groaning, and travailing and I let my request be made known to Him: *Lord, I want to be the youth pastor here, but I want what You want most of all.*

What came in the next few moments and sustained me in those days was a supernatural guarding of my heart and mind. There was no anxiety and I walked in a peace that passed all understanding, reasoning, and feelings. About a month later I was hired, called to be the youth pastor, and entered one of the best seasons of ministry that a person could ever hope for and experience.

Travailing prayer has been talked about very little in most American churches. However, there seems to be a resurgence of this potent prayer theology. I am witnessing leadership gatherings such as New Room Conferences winning back this historic method of prayer. Even publishers, such as Seedbed Publishing, are focusing their printing efforts to help usher in the next great awakening. Doctor David Thomas is a researcher who notes that every great awakening throughout church history was preceded by travailing prayer.[5] These initiatives should be of great interest to every church leader, because it signals that the Lord is prompting people to once again "pray the price" for another great awakening upon our land. Keep your eyes open to this developing story.

7

THE HISTORIC CRY
FOR BOLDNESS

It remains for us to take up courageously
and without hesitation the work He has
given us...

—THOMAS MERTON[1]

Boldness is critical in the arena of evangelism prayer. Bold people pick up the keys of prayer, tenaciously turn those keys in big doors, and expect a big God to come out with some big answers. Timid hearts, on the other hand, feel uncomfortable with that level of authority, even though Jesus gave it to us. Truthfully, whether bold hearts or timid hearts, almost everyone needs to grow in this area of spirituality because the rescue mission has an insatiable need for many bold people praying many bold prayers. In God's worldwide redemption plan, there is no such thing as too many bold prayers opening too many big doors.

Legacy of Boldness

There is a story in 2 Kings 13:14–19 about a conversation between the prophet Elisha and Joash, the king of Israel. Elisha told Joash to take the arrows out of his quiver and smite them on the ground. King Joash did so, and hit the ground three times with the arrows, but then stopped. Elisha was displeased, because the number of times Joash hit the ground was the number of times God would give Israel victory in their battles against Syria. When I read this story, I cannot help but think that God was measuring His interventions for Israel based upon Joash's boldness. If he were of a personality to grab those arrows and smite the ground repeatedly and with great energy, it appears that God would have fought for them in equal measure. Whether Joash was too dignified, too mild, or too uncertain, he was surely anything but bold that day.

The lesson is this: the bold receive more from the inbreaking kingdom of God than do the timid. There is a long history proving that God rushes to flank the bold. Proverbs 28:1 captures the legacy of boldness this way: "The wicked run away when no one is chasing them, but the godly are as bold as lions" (NLT). Whatever one's personality may be, their spiritual identity is to be lion-like and bold because of Christ who lives within us. This is the heritage of God's people, and the very thing that enables God to pour out His plans unabated upon the earth.

The Acts church was linked with boldness over and over again. Even in the face of persecution, it was their boldness that made the world marvel. In Acts 4 alone, there are several repeated instances of boldness. First is in verse 13 when the Sanhedrin saw the boldness of Peter and John and were amazed. Then, in verse 29, their prayers recounted the recent threats of the Jewish leaders but asked for even more boldness to confront the challenge. And, finally, in verse 31, the prayer meeting shook the house as they were all filled with the Spirit and spoke the word of God with boldness. Boldness was the nature of the Acts church. No wonder God responded to them in such great and powerful ways; they were boldly requesting of Him many great things. This is our legacy.

The Greek word most often translated as boldness is *parresia* and can also be translated as fearlessness, courage, or confidence. In the majority of New Testament occurrences, it is connected with speech. It is a demonstrative, powerful, public proclamation by the power of the Holy Spirit. Though not listed in a specific list of the gifts of the Holy Spirit, one can easily connect the idea that our boldness as Christians is rooted in the in-working of the Holy Spirit in a believer's life. It may be more like a mantle we take on as part of our identity in Christ—a descriptor and attribute. Jesus, Peter, Paul, other apostles, and early Christians in general are all characterized by boldness.

I (Jon) was a deputy at a General Convention of the Episcopal Church in 2015. There was a discussion around an amendment to a resolution. The resolution itself was very controversial and the amendment would have been, in my thinking, a better way forward. Ultimately, the amendment was not even considered and was dismissed. I was frustrated and, to be honest, a little angry. That evening I spoke with my bishop, who agreed with me and encouraged me to ask for a point of personal privilege (a parliamentary move to address a body on a topic not necessarily on the agenda). So I did and I wrote out an appropriate yet stern rebuke of the house for shutting down needed dialogue on an important issue. In this context, I sensed the prompting of the Holy Spirit to be bold, to speak out, and to proclaim Christ to a group that was in some ways ignoring the gospel. I'm not sure of all of the outcomes, but I know on several levels it had an effect, as dozens of people sought me out. It also set the stage when other important resolutions came before the house; more time was given to a more thorough discussion.

Built for Adversity

During a vacation this past summer my wife, Melodee, and I (Verlon) went to the Oregon coast. We took a long walk on the beach as the sun was setting. After walking for approximately three miles we turned around to walk back, but there was a surprisingly stiff wind blowing in our face that was not noticeable on the walk down the beach. So we leaned into the wind for our return trip. It was on this return trip that I noticed something interesting: my stride was actually longer going against the wind than it was when the wind was at my back. I was walking over my shoe prints from the journey down the beach, and though they were facing the other direction,

I could see my stride was a full two inches longer facing into the wind. While the stiff wind in my face made me feel like we were walking slower, the fact is we were walking faster. This is a good example of how humans in general handle headwinds in life. Challenges often make us feel like we are going slower or maybe even going backward when, in fact, we are actually walking stronger and faster. Though we long for comfort, we actually thrive more in adversity.

Spiritually speaking, during adversity we lean into the challenge, we lean into sharpening our skills, we lean into our dependency upon God, we lean into prayer, and we lean into boldness. And, surprisingly, we walk stronger, and the kingdom of God gains more ground from us when we are facing a headwind than when we are feeling comfortable. Ecclesiastes 7:14 states that God sends adversity to each of us. Adversity is not a prediction as much as it is a necessity. We must be tested so we learn how to thrive in the day of challenge. This is especially true for those on the frontlines of evangelism. Socrates once said, "A life unexamined is not worth living." We were built to be tested by adversity; do not fear headwinds, stir up your boldness and lean into the conflict. You will learn more about your potential for bold strength than you will ever learn in days of comfort.

You could compare adversity to friction. When friction is geared the right way, it produces energy and movement. Think about sharpening a knife; when you hold it at the proper angle moving it across a stone, the knife's edge gets sharper. If you hold it incorrectly, you can actually dull the knife's edge. As we approach adversity or an obstacle, if we can deal with it in a proper and godly manner, it may actually be turned to our advantage. I penned a song years ago that had these lines:

> *There will be storms, sometimes those waves will roll.*
> *But I'd rather be in the waters with Him than safe*
> *in the harbor alone.*

In all things good or bad, high or low, strong or weak, we have the gift of His abiding presence that will sustain us in all adversity.

Boldness Required

Joshua was the newly appointed commander for the people of Israel. His leadership would be required to activate the troops in a military strategy that was in cooperation with God's miracles. This is seen during the conquest of Jordan: the troops were sent to march around the city, but God needed to knock down the walls. So, Joshua needed to give leadership to military action that was based on miraculous expectancy. This form of leadership required some significant boldness from Joshua. This explains Joshua 1, and the phrase that is repeated four times: "Be strong and of good courage." The human element God needed from Joshua was boldness. That is the same thing the Lord needs from us in prayer; He needs our boldness.

No one opens up doors in heaven without plain old-fashioned human boldness. Many Christians are comfortable praying passive relational prayers, but God is looking for those who can summon their Christian mean streak and pray some bold prayers that move the hand of God. James 5:16 clarifies for us that it is the fervent prayer that is effective and "avails much." Fervency, persistence, and boldness in prayer are what move the hand of God earthward. This is also at the heart of Hebrews 4:16, which directs us to come boldly to the throne of grace that we may obtain answers in the time of need. If we are looking to edify ourselves, then relational prayers are great. But if we are looking to advance the kingdom of God into dark territories, then bold, expectant, declarative prayers are needed. Plainly stated, any expansion of the kingdom of God requires boldness from the people of God.

Boldness Signs Us up for Risky Adventures

Many Christians and leaders desire to be part of something big for God, right up until they realize how much they will have to risk. And then they slump back into a safer version of Christianity. Vince Antonucci laments this all-too-common condition by saying, "We're missing the journey; we're stuck in the same dull routine; we're missing out on the joy and fear and laughter and doubt and mystery and confusion of following Jesus, of taking great risks for God, of praying dangerous prayers."[2] The Christian life is not supposed to be safe, it is supposed to be an adventure. Similarly, Christian prayers are not supposed to merely manage our troubles, they are supposed to sign us up for some risky adventures. Prayer leads to costly action, and radical prayer leads us to boldly risking forward.[3] May our prayers get us into some places that only a miracle from heaven can get us out. That is when our faith is truly alive, and when our role in the God-family rescue mission is life-changing.

There is such a thing as dangerous prayers, which is a prayer-form I (Jon) discovered and ultimately developed into a retreat. These are the prayers that, when you pray them—look out, your life will change. When Moses on the mountain prays, "Show me Your Glory" (Ex. 33:18), he has an encounter that leaves him with a physical manifestation of glowing, so much it scared the Hebrews and he was forced to wear a veil. We could talk about the prayers of Joshua, Gideon, David, Isaiah, Jeremiah, Peter, Paul, and more and how these prayers radically changed the trajectory of their lives. Maybe the most dangerous prayer of all is Mary who, when she hears from the angel of the Lord that she will bear the Messiah, responds with: "Let it be to me according to your word" (Luke 1:38). Prayer itself is a world-changing adventure that is risky and most fulfilling.

Dangerous prayers are anchored in three aspects. There is an *encounter* with almighty God. We enter that thin place of God's presence and we engage and interact with the divine, the weight of His glory manifested. There is a *revelation*. We now know, see, feel, and perceive something we did not know before; a truth has been discovered or deepened in us. Finally, there is a *transformation*. Moses glowed, Peter and Paul got new names, Mary was found with a divine child in her womb. This transformation leads us to confidence and boldness. I would argue that Peter and Paul and others were changed and given a godly boldness to stand and proclaim with authority the gospel throughout the rest of their lives as detailed in the book of Acts.

Boldness Must Be Stirred Up

Every so often, our boldness must be stirred up. Paul did this for young Timothy in 2 Timothy 1:6 when he said, "Stir up the gift of God, which is in you through the laying on of hands." In 2 Peter 1:13 and 3:1, Peter said the same thing two times when he called his readers to stir up their faith.

Sometimes we can stir up our boldness ourselves, but sometimes we need it to be stirred by our brothers and sisters. Often, we are simply too tired or weak to stir it up within ourselves. I see this when Paul finishes his teaching on the armor of God in Ephesians 6:19–20 by asking the Ephesian Christians to pray for him to have more boldness not once, but twice. I am sure that his time in prison and house arrest had worn on him, and though he could teach doctrine with the best of them, the truth is his heart was threadbare at times. Though Paul had warned both the Galatians and the Thessalonian churches not to be weary in well doing (see Galatians 6:9; 2 Thessalonians 3:13), he found himself in exactly that spot—weary in well doing. And so, he reached out for his brothers and sisters to breathe boldness into his soul by their prayers. According to Hebrews 10:24, this is to be the heartbeat of church gatherings: that we will "consider how to stir up one another to love and good works." However we stir up boldness, whether within ourselves or by laying hands on each other in prayer, the church must be found bold. Bold Christians pray bold prayers, and bold prayers are what open big doors.

Attacking the Enemy in Prayer Equates to Winning a Victory on Earth

Only the bold ever attack. Yet, there should be times in every Christian's life when they go on the offensive and make the enemy back down. There are prayers, and then there are "I-have-had-enough-of-this" prayers, in which we turn on our heels and start praying with authority. Tom Clegg says, "Prayer is not preparation for the battle; prayer is the battle."[4] Many Christians shy away from a spiritual battle and certainly shy away from taking an attack posture in prayer. "That is just not my personality," some say. I really like Anne Lamott's response for people who are not natural warriors when she said, "Courage is fear that has said its prayers."[5] Trust me when I say that everyone in the body of Christ has to work at putting on boldness and courage. No one, whatever their personality type, is consistently bold. Every Christian and every Christian leader must learn to put on their Christian mean streak, turn in their tracks, and boldly attack the enemy. May each of us dare to win a great victory for the kingdom of God.

> Be ashamed to die until you have won some victories for humanity.[6]
>
> —HORACE MANN

8

DISPELLING DARKNESS

The rain ceases, and a bird's clear song suddenly announces the difference between Heaven and hell.

—THOMAS MERTON[1]

Another prayer key that opens divine doors is the willingness to dispel darkness. Dealing with the darkness might sound like a scary power encounter of some sort, when actually it is more about turning on the lights of God than facing down Satan. Darkness is dispelled whenever a light switch is flipped. Similarly, the presence of the evil one is dispelled whenever we turn up the presence of the Holy One.

There is something important to be grasped regarding Scripture's metaphor of light. The first creation announcement is: "Let there be light" (Gen. 1:3). Light is a broad element containing various spectrums, the majority of which we do not see with our naked eye. Light contains shortwave radiations; ultra-violet, x-rays, and long-wave radiations; infrared, radio waves, heat, sound, electricity, magnetism, molecular interactions and more. Light is the most basic form of energy.[2] In a spiritual sense, similar to the laws of this physical world, light dispels darkness.

When my (Jon's) grandson Baylor was born, he had a bout of jaundice and the treatment was phototherapy. The Mayo website states:

> A child may be placed under a special lamp that emits light in the blue-green spectrum. The light changes the shape and structure of bilirubin molecules in such a way that they can be excreted in both the urine and stool. During treatment, your baby will wear only a diaper and protective eye patches. Light therapy may be supplemented with the use of a light-emitting pad or mattress.[3]

This is one picture of the power of light to dispel disease and sickness. Imagine the God of all creation working the healing power of light into the mechanics of all that exists. Light and darkness is more than a metaphor, it gets at the heart that almighty God, who dwells in light, shines on us, in us, and through us to bring salvation, deliverance, healing, and all the interventions of His kingdom. This is the mission we are partnering with as we pray.

Authority Gained by Quoting God

One of the great ways to dispel darkness is by the direct use of the words of God. Paul's teaching about the armor of God in Ephesians 6:17 included the sword, which he declared to be the Word of God. It is an amazing insight that the only offensive weapon in Paul's metaphoric teaching is the sword, which is best employed by reciting the words of God.

Quoting God is a powerful activity because it makes the strongman back up. Perhaps this is why Jesus used the words of God exclusively when Satan tempted Him in Luke 4:4–12. Three times Satan offered Jesus the kingdoms of the world, which would have been an easier path than the cross. But in all three instances Jesus answered Satan by quoting Scripture. I am quite sure that the Son of God could have mustered His own words against the evil one, but He limited Himself to quotes from the Father. I surmise that most Christians have not meditated upon the power of the spoken word to disperse darkness. Many read the Bible and they pray, but have they read the Scriptures aloud as their overcoming prayer practice?

Our (Verlon's) church had never considered reading the Scriptures as swordplay, or something that actually stabs at the enemy. But after studying Paul's definition of the sword, we started reading the Psalms aloud as a warfare prayer. Psalm 118 was our first attempt at this, and as we quoted God aloud in prayer, we began to sense that those divine words were thrusting at the enemy and pushing him back. God's authority and presence thickened in the room, while at the same time the cloud of darkness dissipated in the room. If Jesus would use divine quotes to push back the temptations of Satan, why wouldn't we use them too? After a short time, the practice of reading selected God-quotes aloud as a warfare prayer became very meaningful for our church. And in so doing, we learned another key to open up another door in heaven—a door where the light of God pours out and floods the darkness.

I (Jon) once was in the midst of spiritual struggle just over issues that were swirling around my life. My only remedy was God's Word. By memorizing Scriptures, I found comfort, peace, and deliverance. God's promises are true and will sustain us in the midst of conflict or spiritual attack. In the book of Lamentations, the community being referenced was in the midst of great calamity. Read through the first three chapters of Lamentations and you will discover it was a desperate situation. In the midst of threats, poverty, and famine the writer says this: "But this I call to mind, and therefore I have hope: The steadfast love of the LORD never ceases; his mercies never come to an end; they are new every morning; great is your faithfulness" (Lam. 3:21–23).

We call to mind the promises and provision of almighty God to sustain us in all things. The focus, as Verlon said, is not so much on darkness but, rather, on the light of Christ that has come into the world. A favorite text about God's Word offers this encouragement:

> For the word of God is alive and active. Sharper than any double-edged sword, it penetrates even to dividing soul and spirit, joints and marrow; it judges the thoughts and attitudes of the heart. Nothing in all creation is hidden from God's

sight. Everything is uncovered and laid bare before the eyes of him to whom we must give account. (Heb. 4:12–13 NIV)

The Word of God proclaimed, understood, and meditated on shares with us a strength and power to overcome. This is one of my favorite prayers in the *Book of Common Prayer*:

> Blessed Lord, who caused all holy Scriptures to be written for our learning: Grant us so to hear them, read, mark, learn, and inwardly digest them, that we may embrace and ever hold fast the blessed hope of everlasting life, which you have given us in our Savior Jesus Christ; who lives and reigns with you and the Holy Spirit, one God, for ever and ever. Amen.[4]

When we hear, read, mark, learn, and inwardly digest God's Word, it changes our perspective. We get wisdom on how to move forward. We get hope in the midst of calamity. The foundation on which we stand becomes a rock because His Word is alive and active, life-changing, and reorients us to the kingdom.

It is worth referencing again the account of the disciples after Jesus had sent them on a mission. Upon their victorious return, we have this account:

> The seventy-two returned with joy, saying, "Lord, even the demons are subject to us in your name!" And he said to them, "I saw Satan

fall like lightning from heaven. Behold, I have given you authority to tread on serpents and scorpions, and over all the power of the enemy, and nothing shall hurt you. Nevertheless, do not rejoice in this, that the spirits are subject to you, but rejoice that your names are written in heaven." (Luke 10:17–20 ESV)

There was a conflict. Satan lost, yet where did Jesus direct their attention? Answer: that their names were written in heaven. There is a battle to be fought, and yet the rejoicing is directed to what Jesus has already done for us. We win by setting our hearts and minds on almighty God, our Lord and Savior, our defender and hope in all things. We must accurately handle the Word of truth (see 2 Timothy 2:15). We do so from an informed posture standing on the shoulders of the saints, scholars, and theologians through the ages. Scripture lays a firm foundation supporting us in these warfare moments.

The Name of Jesus

Another prayer practice that dispels darkness is to use the name of Jesus. John 1:14 states that Jesus is the Word of God that came and dwelt among us. So, not only is quoting God a manner of using the sword against the evil one, but so is using the name of Jesus in an authoritative manner. If you want an interesting Bible study, look up how many times "the name of Jesus" is cited by the early believers in the New Testament—especially in the book of Acts. James White states that the prime characteristic of these early Christian prayers seems to be that they were voiced in the name of Jesus.[5] They clearly understood that the name of Jesus was what authorized them to function in the antagonistic Roman and Gentile environments. Beyond the book of Acts, the tradition of praying in the name of Jesus continued. I love Paul's opening reminder in 1 Corinthians 1:2, that everyone and in every place should remember to call on the name of Jesus. When the first church called on the name of Jesus, they were calling forth the works of Christ that were still near and dear in their memories. Prayers that called on Jesus were prayers that called forth healing, salvation, and victory over the works of the enemy. Oh, that more of our prayers today would call on the name of Jesus rather than using it as a perfunctory sign-off to signify the prayer is ending. There is great power when we use that name; power to open doors in heaven and power to close down dark corridors on earth.

When we began leaning into the dinner table theology in Seattle, our research of the Apostolic Era revealed that preaching was not like what we are used to today. The first apostles stayed focused on the stories of Christ and the stories Christ told. Even Paul said in 2 Timothy 4:3 that when he preached it wasn't like the populous teachers of his day. Instead, it was what he reported in 1 Corinthians 1:23, that he just preached Christ and Him crucified. In fact, Paul's preaching focused on the stories of Christ so simply that he was criticized as being too plain. But Paul wore this rebuke with honor in 1 Corinthians 2:4 because his Christ-centric preaching ushered in the "power of God." And that is exactly why the name of Jesus is so important.

We just cannot talk about Jesus enough, both in conversation and in prayer. Let's take a moment to soak in the historic prayer of St. Patrick:

"Christ beside me, Christ before me, Christ behind me, Christ within me, Christ beneath me, and Christ above me."[6]

The name of Jesus is to be cherished and, more so, embraced as a comfort and protection. We invoke the name of Jesus in spiritual warfare because He is the Christus Victor! The name of Jesus has power because He defeated death and won eternal salvation for those who believe in Him. There is now a victory for every Christian over darkness and death in the name of Jesus.

This Jesus is the stone that was rejected by you, the builders, which has become the cornerstone. And there is salvation in no one else, for there is no other name under heaven given among men by which we must be saved. (Acts 4:11–12 ESV)

When we come by faith and repentance to Jesus, we are given this brand. Like the St. Patrick prayer, the name of Jesus is spoken over, under, beside, behind, before, and within me and yields a comprehensive salvation experience in every way imagined.

Presencing Worship

Worship has historically been held as a significant battle plan. Most of the church today would be surprised to learn that worshiping together has been conceived as spiritual warfare by many of our heroes in the faith. In Judges 20:18, Israel was facing a civil war against the tribe of Benjamin. When the other eleven tribes gathered to confront Benjamin, they paused to ask God which tribe was to march first into battle. God answered them by indicating Judah should go first. Judah, which means worship, was to be the point of the spear in this battle. This battle turned out to be very difficult, in which it took three separate attack campaigns to finally win. But God wanted worship to lead the way. Similarly, in Joshua 3:6–17 when the nation of Israel was facing the Jordan River at flood stage, it was the priests carrying the ark of the covenant who stepped into the water first. When they did, the torrential waters started backing up so that they actually stood on dry ground in the middle of the river. The priests, the worship leaders of the assembly who were carrying the ark representing the presence of God, brought a miraculous victory for Israel over a flooding river. Then just a few chapters later in Joshua 6:20, when Israel faced the walled city of Jericho, they worshipped their way around the wall for seven days in a row. And on the seventh day, the walls fell down flat and opened up the city to them. Once again, it was worship that gave them the decisive victory and created a reputation of miraculous power as they entered the promised land. The idea of winning battles with worship should not be foreign to Bible readers. Similarly, the idea of dispelling darkness by worship should not feel foreign either.

Psalm 22:3 declares that "You are holy, Enthroned in the praises of Israel." Which means that when we lift up verbal praises about our God, His presence inhabits that place and makes it His throne. This is what "presencing" worship is about. While some people think worship is an act of obedience, and others think worship is to edify the worshiper, actually it far more potent than that. It opens up a divine door in which the presence of the Lord flows onto earth. In light of scriptural history, it is not difficult to see why worship wins battles over the strongman and dispels darkness upon the earth.

Our dinner churches in Seattle use presencing worship as a central part of our evenings. Our dinners often have a significant percentage of people with life-controlling issues and obvious brokenness. But when our worship leaders begin to sing the deep and reverent worship songs of the church, a peaceful and healing Spirit sweeps into the room. Sometimes people will push their food back, turn their chair to see the worship leaders, and start wiping tears from their eyes. While people raised with secular world-views do not sing like church folks do, they will sit and cry while we sing. We often hear from visiting people who work with nonprofits in other communities that there are fights and conflicts on a regular basis, and they marvel that in our rooms there is peace. The reason for this is simple: our worship is presencing Christ into the room, while at the same time dispelling the voice of darkness.

It is interesting to note that when Jesus was teaching His disciples how to pray in Matthew 6:9, He directed them to worship first. Even before He taught them to pray, "Thy kingdom come," He taught them to pray, "Holy be Thy name." He was teaching them a divine progression; it is valuable to usher in the presence of God before doing other spiritual business.

We see a heavenly glimpse of this prayer-form in Revelation 4:8, where the created worship beings repeat the phrase "Holy, Holy, Holy" without rest day and night in recognition of the presence of God. Paul and Silas discovered the potency of worship to not only break spiritual chains but actual chains in Acts 16:25–26. They were cuffed and locked in prison and were undoubtedly encouraging themselves by singing worship songs to the Lord. But as they sang, a divine shaking occurred that opened the prison doors and broke the cuffs off of their feet and hands. This was not a stand-alone miracle for us to marvel at; those prison doors flew open for a reason. Their worship drew in God's presence and stifled the strongman's ability to hold these two evangelists. Make no mistake: worship is warfare.

Ultimately, the whole of the Bible is all about the presence of the Lord. We were created to be in His presence. The Westminster Shorter Catechism begins with this:

Q: What is the chief end of man?
A: Man's chief end is to glorify God, and to enjoy him forever.[7]

When this relationship with God was broken by sin, the rest of Bible tells us the story of how this relationship is restored. God is a covenant God and all the covenants seek humanity's reconciliation with almighty God. The promise comes again and again throughout the Bible. In Exodus 6:7 (ESV) it says, "I will take you to be my people, and I will be your God, and you shall know that I am the LORD your God, who has brought you out from under the burdens of the Egyptians." And Scripture repeats this covenantal statement numerous times (see Genesis 17:7; Ezekiel 36:28; Jeremiah 7:23; 30:22; 31:33).

God seeks us out to be our defender, protector, our Lord, and King. The promise in Psalm 23 is His presence: "Yea, though I walk through the valley of the shadow of death, I will fear no evil: *for thou art with me*; thy rod and thy staff they comfort me" (Ps. 23:4 KJV, emphasis added). We fear not because of His presence. This is such an important truth for us to keep in our hearts that Jesus' final words at the end the Great Commission before He ascended were: "Surely, I am with you always, to the very end of the age" (Matt. 28:20 NIV).

This promise of God's presence is paramount. There are possibly no more comforting words than these regarding this issue from Romans 8:31–39 (ESV):

> What then shall we say to these things? If God is for us, who can be against us? He who did not spare his own Son but gave him up for us all, how will he not also with him graciously give us

all things? Who shall bring any charge against God's elect? It is God who justifies. Who is to condemn? Christ Jesus is the one who died—more than that, who was raised—who is at the right hand of God, who indeed is interceding for us. Who shall separate us from the love of Christ? Shall tribulation, or distress, or persecution, or famine, or nakedness, or danger, or sword? As it is written, "For your sake we are being killed all the day long; we are regarded as sheep to be slaughtered." No, in all these things we are more than conquerors through him who loved us. For I am sure that neither death nor life, nor angels nor rulers, nor things present nor things to come, nor powers, nor height nor depth, nor anything else in all creation, will be able to separate us from the love of God in Christ Jesus our Lord.

Psalm 139:7 (NIV) declares: "Where can I go from your Spirit? Where can I flee from your presence?" We usher in His felt presence with praise and worship. Often attributed to St. Augustine is this quote: "He who sings prays twice." When we lift our voice in prayer and adoration, we add melody and cadence so there can come an anointing and the felt presence of the Lord. As a musician and worship leader for most of my life, I know this personally and corporately. Worshiping God becomes a conduit for His power and presence.

The Disinvite/Invite Principle

Though the enemy is the prince and power of the air, every resident of earth has the right to determine the spiritual atmosphere that they want inhabiting their life, their home, their family, and their ministries. Which means that each of us has the power to disinvite some things from our lives and invite other things into our lives. Paul was speaking to this to the Corinthian people in 2 Corinthians 4:2 when he reminded them that they had renounced hidden things, craftiness, and deceitfulness. This verse has become, for some, the prayer of renouncement. In other words, there is transformative power in disinviting some sinful behaviors and the spiritual influences that informed those behaviors. Once understood, this prayer gives us the opportunity to actually disinvite the strongman and his works of darkness from our hearts, homes, ministries, and neighborhoods.

To disinvite something creates the opportunity to invite a healthier replacement. Jesus spoke to this in Matthew 12:43–45, where He told the story of the man who disinvited a dark spirit but did not fill the space in his soul with anything better. Then the dark spirit came back with seven other spirits and overwhelmed the man so that the last state of the man's life was worse than before. Jesus did not tell this story to scare people, but rather to teach the disinvite/invite principle, and the necessity of filling the void with the Spirit of God. To disinvite the spirit of fear, or infirmity, or lust, or greed, and then invite the Spirit of

Christ and Christ alone is a powerful way to gain mastery over the evil one. This is a great prayer for those trying to get free from pornography or other inward addictions. This is actually an interesting way to understand the theological term of "consecration." Consecration means to give ourselves solely and completely to Christ and His ways. The prayer of invite compels the Spirit of Christ and Him alone into our hearts, our homes, our ministries, and our neighborhoods. To pray a disinvite prayer followed by an invite prayer is a powerful way to flood the darkness with divine light. If you do not want the spirit of darkness hanging around your story—disinvite it. If you want the spirit of Christ immersing your story—invite Him. We get what we pray for.

A gentleman that attends one of our (Verlon's) dinner churches in Seattle told me he had stopped using heroin in the past few months. I was amazed and asked him how. He looked at me with a baffled look on his face and said, "You guys did it!" To which I replied, "But none of us even knew you had a heroin problem. How did we do it?" He then reported that every time he came into our dinner church room, the heroin voice would leave him, and would not come back for three days. Further, whenever the voice returned, all he had to do was hold off the temptation until five o' clock and catch a bus to whichever neighborhood was serving a dinner church that night. And after three months of running into our rooms whenever he felt tempted, the voice left him and has not returned.

So, what was actually happening in this man's story? The disinvite/invite principle was at work. We had flooded our dinner church rooms with such light that the voice of darkness simply could not come in with this man. He could come into our dinners, but the spirit of darkness could not. The light of Christ's presence ushered in by our worship, preaching, serving, and praying simply overwhelmed the dark voice trying to talk to him. I have seen parents use this same principle to pray through their house, and especially the room of their rebellious teen. And later in the day have that child walk into the house only to watch their hard, angry, sullen, and hateful attitude dissipate as they entered. Those parents had disinvited the works of darkness in their home. The child could enter; the darkness could not. The effectiveness of the disinvite/invite prayer has a wonderful ability to dispel the works of darkness that are oppressing individuals, families, and ministries.

Prayer and Swords

The presence of swords in Paul's list of armor in Ephesians 6:11 means something; it assumes that we will attack back at some point in our Christian experience. The clouds of darkness that arise from time to time are an offensive strategy the strongman uses to suppress God's people. But these are the moments that men and women of God attack back. Robert Anderson stated: "Attack conflict with prayer."[8] In other words, we recognize these clouds and conflicts are common enemies for those in the rescue business. So, when those conflicts show up, we pull out our swords and we attack. James 4:7 states: "Resist the devil and he will flee from you." Wielding our swords is part of our Christian duty, especially for Christians on the frontlines of evangelism. Darrel Guder says it well: "The church must see itself as participating in God's victory over evil."[9] Perhaps there will be a day when we catch ourselves praying this preacher's prayer: "Oh Lord, give me someone to save, and a devil to stab. Amen."

9

THE UNPARALLELED POWER OF PRAYER WALKS

Everything in modern city life is calculated
to keep man from . . . thinking about
spiritual things.

—THOMAS MERTON[1]

There is a particular key that is quite potent in down-loading God's presence into neighborhoods—the prayer walk. Some people walk and pray because it keeps them focused on the task, but that is not the same thing as walking through a particular neighborhood and asking God to flood those streets with increased grace, favor, and blessing. The most powerful form of prayer walking, when properly understood, is akin to claiming a new territory for God's kingdom and ushering in His prevailing presence.

Ancient Prayer Walks

In Deuteronomy 11:24 we read these words: "Every place on which the sole of your foot treads shall be yours . . . shall be your territory." While this was God's way of giving the children of Israel their promised land, it also reveals the way God thinks about His children and the territories of the earth. This is repeated again in Joshua 1:3–4: "Every place that the sole of your foot *will* tread upon I have given you . . . shall be your territory" (emphasis added). I really like the progression of the promise. When it was first offered it was a conceptual promise, but when they stood on the edge of entering the promised land, it added the word *will*. What this suggests is that the very act of walking into their promised land was the activity by which they would receive their promised land. Thus, as they walked in, God handed over territory to His people. We need a restoration of this ancient understanding today.

The theological backdrop of the prayer walk, then, is that we can actually convert territory that has been prevailed over by the prince of the air into territory that is now prevailed over by the kingdom of God. By placing the soles of our feet in neighborhoods, streets, and houses and declaring, "Yours, Lord," we are following the same pattern God told the children of Israel to use at the attainment of their promised land. Do we think that the promised land given in the days of Moses was the only promised land God has ever apportioned? I believe that the Lord is still willing to delegate territory to every ministry functioning today. However, not every ministry recognizes how intentionally they have been sent to an area and to a people, to call forth the kingdom of God upon them. While this understanding and activity never usurps the will of any person living there, a church can certainly increase the prevailing presence of Christ in their neighborhood. And this is the power of prayer walks. Step by step, God's people have brought territories under God's influence for centuries. And that ancient way still works.

Neighborhood Churches Pray Neighborhood Prayers

Ever since the church growth movement of the 1960s, we have been overly affected by the regional church concept. While I spoke about this in an earlier chapter, it bears repeating. The church of Jesus was conceived as a neighborhood church throughout Christian history, but the regional church vision and the fifteen-minute driving circle has eclipsed the neighborhood identity in our lifetime. Accordingly, the close relational connections that have inspired the prayers of the church for centuries have been eclipsed; many church attenders find themselves praying diffused prayers over large nameless areas rather than specific needs in the neighborhood that they walk through and the neighbors they know on a first-name basis. It is tough to muster compelling evangelistic prayers for nameless areas; it is quite easy to contend for the souls of people when we know them by name and feel their pain because of our friendship with them. This is the great strength of the neighborhood church.

The theology of place is making a resurgence in these days, which is reminding the church that God is very interested in particular locations and the particular people living in those areas. Further, the theology of place is helping churches regain a sense of calling to certain people-circles and restore the potency of the historic neighborhood church. Neighborhood churches that learn to pray compelling prayers for their neighborhoods are often drawn by the Spirit to walk and pray through their neighborhoods. And, in so doing, they increase the presence of Christ on their streets and in the lives of their neighbors.

I (Jon) have rediscovered the power of prayer walking in the last few years. A ministry I took on a few years back was crumbling and in shambles. With few resources, the only thing I could do was pray. So, I began two to three times a week walking over the property, praying for the darkness to be dispersed, and for the light of Christ to shine on these acres. I prayed for provision, protection, and guidance. I prayed for the staff and people we ministered to, for wisdom and vision for a future. God answered those prayers! The ministry was righted and reestablished; we began to bear real fruit in the work we were called to. We became financially stable and sustainable. What had been hanging by a thread was now strong and growing.

Prayer walking is an essential module in Fresh Expressions training. It is a part of Vision Days, Learning

Communities, Roundtables, and more. In Learning Communities that train Pioneers to do Fresh Expressions, one of the most fruitful moments is actually doing a prayer walk in the community during their training. The stories the pioneers come back with are truly inspiring and invariably become the highlight of the two-day training sessions.

I (Jon) recently took on a new vocation as a part-time priest in a small, rural, coastal community. I am starting my leadership task by doing prayer walks in this new community, praying to God: "What are You already doing here? Who is here? Where are the people of peace who will open doors for mission and ministry? Please give me favor, wisdom, and discernment. Show me the mission and ministry You want to launch in this place. Bring people alongside to prayer walk with me as we pray for this community." Based on previous experience, I fully expect the Lord to open doors to me as I walk and pray.

Long before we initiate any new thing, before we start a new program or begin a new work, we will pray and have agreement as to what we are to do. In the first movie in the Jurassic Park franchise, the fictional director of the park, John Hammond, is explaining how they recreated the dinosaurs. Scientist and philosopher Dr. Ian Malcolm responds: "Yeah, but your scientists were so preoccupied with whether or not they *could* that they didn't stop to think if they *should*." I call this the Jurassic Park Principle. Sometimes the church does this. We get so enamored with the latest program, ministry concept, or piece of technology that we rush in with trying to make it happen without taking the time to ask: Should we?

In theology we talk about *eisegesis* and *exegesis*. These terms usually refer to how a person would interpret Scriptures. They can be expanded to how a person interprets a variety of things, including culture. Eisegesis is the process of interpreting in such a way as to introduce one's own presuppositions, agendas, or biases. We come with assumptions and act on them as though they are true. The church has long practiced this. We start a ministry, spend money and resources, even build a building for something that may not even be needed. We do so, thinking we know best. I have been guilty of this. With more than thirty years of ministry experience, I have a bag of tricks—things I've done in the past with great success. I could launch a dozen ministries and programs all at once, and they could be good things to do. However, should I? A wise matriarch taught me years ago: Do not let the good become the enemy of the best. There are a lot of good things to do, but what are the very best things God is calling you to do? If you do a lot of good things, you will get too busy and can miss the best things.

Exegesis of a community is to examine, discern, and understand what is here. What are the contexts, values, and dreams of the people in this place? We don't bring our conjectures or guesses as to the cultural content. We see what is there and take note. Prayer is the major way we do exegesis. We look and listen prayerfully to our surroundings and, by listening to the Holy Spirit, we perceive the next step. In prayer walks, we discover the best things to do.

In the Fresh Expressions movement, we teach how to form a new faith community by using the Five Circles Discernment Process. The first step, before anything else, is to listen! This is an activity of prayer more than anything else. Interestingly, by the time we get to the end of the Discernment Process training, the students realize that each of the Five Circles are undergirded by continual and ongoing prayer.

One aspect I love about prayer walks is the connection to an ancient practice. In Scripture, as well as things practiced in the past centuries like rogation and beating the bounds, we are aligning to previous leaders and seasons in the faith. When we engage in prayer walks, we do not do them alone, but are joined by a "great cloud of witnesses" (Heb. 12:1) and the communion of saints who are cheering us on. I have an appreciation for churches that have cemeteries beside them. They serve as a constant reminder that we are surrounded and what we do in this life is not done in a vacuum. Rather, our faith and prayers are being practiced in the fellowship of the saints who have gone before. My friend Steve Fry wrote a song years ago, "I'm Abandoned," with these verses:

We've been raised for such a time,
Hist'ry comes to the finish line
And the saints who've gone before,
Watch to see us end our course

So lay aside each weight that binds,
And enter in the harvest time
Until the kingdoms of this world,
Become the Kingdoms of our Christ[2]

Breathing Blessing

One of the great things to do while on a prayer walk is to breathe blessing on the neighborhood and the people who live there with every step. Alvin Vander Griend reports that their Houses of Prayer direct prayer teams to pray five blessings on five neighbors in five minutes, five days a week.[3] Praying blessing into a neighborhood is a powerful thing. Just speaking the word *blessing* upon people, streets, apartment buildings, businesses, and community centers ushers Christ's presence into public spaces. Further, such prayers leave a resonance of divine warmth in the wake of where people have prayer walked. Often when I am prayer walking, I find myself uttering words under my breath like *blessing*, *favor*, *outpouring*, *goodness*, and *healing* over and over again as I walk. When I do this, I can sense grace flowing from heaven and changing the very atmosphere of the sidewalks that I am walking on. And similar to how Jesus saw Satan fall like lightning (see Luke 10:18), I feel blessing falling onto the streets and into the lives of the neighbors and dispelling darkness. Never discount the power of the word *blessing* to open a great door in heaven and affect a particular location on earth.

A few years ago, I (Jon) was with a group of senior church leaders and they were being asked questions about life. These seven giants of the faith were all sharing the wisdom they had garnered from more than three hundred years of collective ministry experience. (You would recognize their names if I told you; I was simply honored to be in the room!) One of these leaders told us that he had one large desire emerge in his life: to bless people and speak blessing over lives, young and old alike. His words were so compelling as he spoke of blessing that I knew I was in the presence of something great that day. I determined to be a conduit of blessing day by day with the people I meet. I now sign most of my e-mails with a simple word—*Blessings.* It may be a small thing, but I have learned that God uses small things when there is a righteous intent behind them.

Praying in the Spirit

Prayer walks are a great time to pray in the Spirit. In Ephesians 6:18, Paul told the church to "pray in the Spirit at all times and on every occasion" (NLT). I realize that praying in the Spirit means different things for different denominations, but prayer walks beg for this form of prayer to be released. Praying in the Spirit downloads things from heaven into a neighborhood that is beyond the knowledge of the people doing the praying. There are many deep challenges going on in our neighborhoods that we could not possibly know anything about, but the

Spirit who lives within us does. And as we walk, the Spirit intercedes through us.

On a recent prayer walk we walked silently and separate from each other. We gathered back together afterward and I (Jon) asked: "What did you see, hear, or feel?" One person mentioned they saw buildings that were old and in various stages of decay. This became a parable for us, as we saw these buildings representing a deeper spiritual, emotional, moral decay in our community. This download gave us direction and focus in our prayers for our community.

You can learn to pray in the Spirit without having to declare that you are a Pentecostal. There might be cultural elements of Pentecostalism that you are not comfortable with. However, if you desire to breathe powerful interventions into your neighborhood, you might want to step past those fears and learn to pray in the Spirit in ways that are comfortable for you. One researcher reports in 2007 that half of his denomination's pastors believe that praying privately "in the Spirit" is biblical, though their official doctrinal statements did not make room for that.[4] Here is the big reveal: many Christian leaders feel the need to pray in the Spirit—far more than is ever talked about. If you are feeling compelled to engage in prayer walks, I'd recommend finding a way to pray in the Spirit. We do this by allowing the Holy Spirit to guide us in our prayers through thoughts, stirrings, words, observations, and deeds.

This could be a whole other book, but we need to get better acquainted with the Holy Spirit. In the church we talk a lot about knowing Jesus and the Father—as we should. It is, after all, a relationship. We need to approach the Holy Spirit in the same way and learn the ways of this distinct member of the Trinity. The more we dwell in and with the Spirit, the more we are able to be empowered and effective in the mission of the church. The Holy Spirit is what distinguishes us as the church. The early church did not have what we have today in terms of buildings, budgets, staff, and the like. But the early church functioned in the power of the Holy Spirit like Jesus did, and that made people take notice. There are a lot of things we believe are necessary for the life of the church, but, in reality, many of those things are simply traditions. I would challenge us all to consider the church as it was in the book of Acts—a faith community doing life together in the Spirit.

I am drawn to this summary statement in Acts 9:31 (ESV): "So the church throughout all Judea and Galilee and Samaria had peace and was being built up. And walking in the fear of the Lord and in the comfort of the Holy Spirit, it multiplied." Notice the descriptions: peace, being built up, walking in the fear of the Lord, and the comfort of the Holy Spirit leading to growth and multiplication. This is the normative model for church that we are missing in many places.

Now let me hasten to say that I prefer people not praying loudly during their walks, laying their hands on buildings, or making a public spectacle of their prayer practices. In 1 Corinthians 14:23 Paul warns about not using spiritual gifts and prayer-forms in a way that confuses and disturbs lost people. Paul would direct us to shape the use of our spiritual gifts to fit the social environment we are in. When on a sidewalk, there are social assumptions that we need to honor. So, let us do our prayer walks while praying under our breaths. The power of these prayer activities is not diminished because they are not done in volume or a visible demonstration of spirituality. Rather, the power of prayer walks flows from ushering Christ into our neighborhoods. I (Verlon) am a lifelong Pentecostal, but I appeal to all of my brothers and sisters to do your prayer walks in ways that onlookers only see you walking, not praying. The Lord who is looking on the heart knows full well you are opening up heaven's doors as you walk, and that is what matters.

Praying in the Spirit is a potent activity that changes things and contends for souls in ways other prayer-forms cannot. Saint Seraphim of Sarov spoke of this in 1833 when he said, "But only acquire the Holy Spirit and you will save a thousand around you."[5] Praying in the Spirit as we walk affects a thousand needs and perhaps even a thousand people. That is no small thing.

Here, Lord, Here!

True to our heritage, we have the opportunity to pour God's interventions into our neighborhoods with every step we take, which is the theological backbone of the prayer walk. When we walk our streets and usher in

God's outpouring, we are partnering with one of Christ's great desires. Abraham Kuyper's most frequently quoted passage is: "There is not a square inch in the whole domain of our human existence over which Christ . . . does not cry: 'Mine!'"[6] When I am engaged in prayer walks, I feel like I am answering Christ's great desire to wrap His arms around people and places. I find great power in praying, "Yours, Lord, Yours," and, "Here, Lord, Here." Prayer walks are the greatest of opportunities to hold the door open for Christ and increase His influence in a neighborhood. May the neighborhood of your calling become greatly favored as you walk those streets and cry, "Come, Lord, Come"; "Here, Lord, Here"; "Yours, Lord, Yours!"

10

THE LEAST, THE LAST, AND THE LEFT BEHIND

> Those who abandon everything in order to seek God know well that He is the God of the poor.
>
> —THOMAS MERTON[1]

There is a key to prayer that understands a particular soft spot in the heart of Jesus. Praying for favor to flood into the lives of the poor is one prayer that is central to our Lord's passion. When Jesus walked on the earth, He unapologetically preferred the poor, as evidenced by the use of His time. This means something. And it is an important understanding for us as we deepen in our prayer practices.

Helpless

One of the great oversights of many Americans is assuming that the lower third can change their situation if they just want to. There is no doubt that a good work ethic is better than a bad one, but it is not a silver bullet that benefits every person equally. People who live in lower-third neighborhoods do not have the same opportunities that the middle-class locations offer. There are many things in the families and lives of lower-third neighborhoods that confuse one's work ethic and disable a person's desire to move up the economic ladder. Support systems that are natural in middle- and upper-class locations, the kind that nurture optimism and a good work ethic, are usually absent in lower-third neighborhoods. Most Americans underappreciate the doors that fly open for them as a result of clean clothes, good teeth, good haircuts, and a conversational ability that has been practiced in a world of prosperity. However, many lower-third Americans have an underlying sense of hopelessness and stifled work ethic simply because they were raised in families and neighborhoods that could not offer these supports. Regardless of opportunity, there will be people who will ignore the way out and continue to choose poverty because it is what they know. The reality is that people choose this also because, on one level, it is a choice they can make.

Any church would be enriched if they spent some time noticing and weeping for the neighbors near them who are being crushed by economic challenges. The book of Job is painful in many ways, but I like where he defended himself in Job 30:25 (KJV) by saying, "Did I not weep for him that was in trouble? And was not my soul grieved for the poor?" If Jesus were to show up in the lower-third neighborhoods of our country, we would witness what the disciples saw in Matthew 9:36—a Jesus who is moved with compassion over the lost and wandering peoples.

While it is degrading and socially unacceptable to declare out loud that our neighbors are helpless, the truth is many are without options. And this understanding should motivate the people of God to prayer and action. Thomas Merton wrote: "God, who is infinitely rich, became man in order to experience the poverty and misery of fallen man, not because He needed this experience but because we needed His example."[2] Christ has given us a great example of how to do life on this earth, and it is an example that includes large investments of time, tears, grief, compassion, and prayer for the poor. Shall we be like Him? If our answer is yes, it will focus our prayer lives in the direction of the poor and the broken.

Motivated by Mercy

Jesus is motivated by mercy. It is an easy thing to offer prayers without remembering the motives of the one we are directing our prayers toward. However, it is an empowering thing to know our Lord's deepest motivation for answering our prayers. Jesus revealed the divine motivation in Luke 11:11–13 (NLT): "If your children ask for a fish, do you give them a snake instead? Of if they ask for an egg, do you give them a scorpion? And if you sinful people know how to give good gifts to their children, how much more will the heavenly Father give?" Jesus made it clear that heaven feels certain sensitivity to our needs when we pray. This should give us confidence. Hebrews 4:15–16 states that Jesus understands our weakness because He faced them too, which means that we should come boldly to the throne of grace in our time of need. Christ's sympathy is the greatest reason for our confidence in prayer.

The Eastern church holds to a practice of prayer called the Kyrie Eleison, which is a prayer offered in view of the true heart of Jesus, "Lord, have mercy." These have become the most repeated words in Eastern liturgy in which they recognize that the deepest motivation of Christ is mercy for the plight of humanity.[3] Once we see mercy as the prime motivation of Christ, it not only affects our prayer confidence, it affects our desire to lift the least of these.

People from numerous backgrounds have noted an important correlation between their care for the poor and the quality of their lives. As an example, there is a line in the New Revised Standard Version's Sirach 3:30 that teaches how almsgiving delivers from death and purges away every sin.[4] Offering mercy to others increases our ability to receive mercy for ourselves, enabling us to drive away the carnal desires that seek to destroy us. This is even more true for Christ-followers. Many American Christians would be surprisingly blessed by leaning into the mercy of Christ for the least, the last, and the left behind. In doing so, not only would the poor be lifted, but also the saints would increase their confidence in prayer. Simply stated, the church needs the poor to help us develop our confidence in the mercy-filled Christ.

While lifting the poor should be normal, many churches have spent the bulk of their time ministering to the middle- and upper-class congregants. In this day, it is popular for church leaders to be informed by demographics, but Jesus was mostly informed by socioeconomics. This should be a very sober point of meditation. Whether it was Jesus' eye for the widows' offering in Luke 21:2, His stories about inviting the poor to great banquets in Matthew 22:9, or the sheer volume of Gospel verses that capture Jesus spending time with the poor, He directed much of His ministry through the lens of socioeconomics. We need to look again at our towns and neighborhoods through Christ's eyes, His mercy-filled eyes. In so doing, we will not only change our churches, but we will learn to assume mercy, mercy, and more mercy in our prayers—a legitimate social justice fueled by gospel intention and love for others. The poor are a means of encounter—a thin place. "Inasmuch as you did to one of the least of these My brethren, you did it to Me" (Matt. 25:40).

Prayer walks are a call to see some things; to understand the context and the world in which we live. And this is important because we tend to grow blind to the things we pass by every day. There is a long list of Jesus' seeing people and being interrupted by their need. He saw the woman with an issue of blood, the widow of

Nain, the blind and lame, lepers, and infirm. We need to pray in a way to see things like Jesus did.

The duty of a Christian is to give our time, talent, and treasure. In Matthew 10:7–8 we find this instruction as Jesus sends out the disciples on mission: "As you go, preach, saying, 'The kingdom of heaven is at hand.' Heal the sick, cleanse the lepers, raise the dead, cast out demons. *Freely you have received, freely give*" (emphasis added). We are not to be a pool that gathers water with no flow and becomes stagnant and dead. Rather, we are to be a river or stream, a conduit of God's mercy, kindness, and provision to the world. We take what we have received, and we share.

Confronting Injustice

I love the story in Exodus 17:10, where Moses climbed to the top of a hill that overlooked the battleground where Israel was attacked by the Amalekites. It was not a fair fight because Amalek had trained warriors while Israel's men were only skilled in making bricks. It is no surprise, then, why the warriors of Amalek were defeating the men of Israel quite handily. That was until Moses climbed up the hill and raised the rod of the Lord over his head. When he did that, the men of Israel gained a divinely infused fighting ability and began to defeat the stronger and better-equipped Amalekite warriors. What Moses was doing was instituting God's authority over the battle. He was calling God to intervene in an unjust situation; he was enacting the Old Testament equivalent of "Thy kingdom come."

The people of God have within our heritage both the calling and the ability to institute the authority of God in unjust situations. Richard Stearns stated that we are commanded by Christ to go into the world—to bear fruit by lifting up the poor and challenging injustice wherever we find it.[5] Paul reminded the church in 1 Corinthians 13:6 that love stops rejoicing when injustice is present. We are the people on the earth who abhor injustice when it presses against our neighbor. But sometimes we need to be reminded of that righteous commitment.

I like the Latin American Prayer: "Oh God, to those who have hunger give bread; and to those who have bread give the hunger for justice."[6] Every church needs to consider the question: Do we have a hunger for justice? If we can walk by the poor without feeling the pangs of their situation, we might need to pray that our hunger for justice be restored. Often our hunger for justice lags because we have located our churches and our lives a safe distance from the lower-third neighborhoods. It is not only possible, but likely that we worship, study Scriptures, and enjoy Christian fellowship in a sanitized middle- to upper-class atmosphere. This creates distance from the need of the broken and the pain of the poor. When we do this, our prayers become nameless, painless, and passionless. Thomas Merton addressed this sanitized distance problem by saying, "Do not ask me to love my brother merely in the name of an abstraction like loving society, the human race, or the common good."[7] There are many prayers sent heavenward by good people who are trying to do right by society, but their prayers are not as powerful as they could be, because they are not rooted in the pain of injustice.

Praying powerful authoritative prayers in the face of injustice is wonderful, but it is not the end-all. Our prayers might have an opportunity to turn into action. Some misunderstand that progression. Using prayer to escape action is not the historic way; rather, employing prayer while readying our hands for action is the age-old pattern of Christianity. Prayer is a two-way endeavor in which we ask God to answer our prayers, and correspondently He asks us to answer His. When we contend for justice for those around us, we might be asked to be a part of the divine intervention.

Some churches have felt called to arise and defend a certain people group that are trapped in a societal inequity. While such a response should never consume the church's identity, it is a wonderful thing when the Lord calls His people to stand up for oppressed people in prayer and action. Desmond Tutu is a Christian leader who has spent his ministry in the dark shadow of numerous injustices, and gives this important warning: "We should spend as much time in prayer as we spend in protest."[8] Tempering our protests with prayer not only adds power to our efforts, but also provides divine protection from getting swept up in emotionally charged revolts that are beyond the Lord's calling for us. May our first battle against injustice be won in the courts of heaven before they are won in the courts of man!

Beholding Jesus

There is a very close relationship between being with Jesus and being with the poor. It is the nature of Jesus to be with those who need Him most, so if we will be close to Him as He walks the earth, it is likely we will be close to the broken sectors of humanity. In Matthew 25:35–40, Jesus said that when we feed the poor, include the stranger, care for the sick, and visit the prisoner we are actually doing it to Him. By this, He was indicating that His proximity to the broken is so close that when we are with them, we cannot help but be with Him. Mother Teresa spoke to this by saying, "In the faces of the poor I have seen Christ in his most distressing disguise."[9] The closest we will ever be to the presence of Jesus is not in church sanctuaries, but rather in the sore neighborhoods while we are lifting the poor and the broken. Dick Foth suggested that if any church ever loses Jesus, they should go the poor, because the poor will lead them back to Him. There is an undeniable connection between Christ-centric spirituality and spending time with the poor.

There are some historic descriptors that need to be added again in this day to define mission. What sets authentic Christianity apart, our greatest witness, is the degree to which we love. Jesus said people would know that we are His disciples because of the love we have for one another (see John 13:34–35). The early church's profound witness to Roman society was the love it had not only for other Christians, but a love, compassion, and kindness extended to those who lived on the margins— the vulnerable and needy, widows, and orphans.

If I were to paraphrase the apostle John's writings, it would sound like this:

> Little children, do you not know God is love? We know what love is because He loved us, and Jesus gave His life on a cross for us. I was there. I saw this love with my own eyes! Love held Him to the cross. He didn't have to do this, but He did because He loves us. Let me tell you about His love! He embraced sinners, foreigners, traitors, enemies, the lame, the deaf, and the blind! I wrote in my Gospel: "In the beginning was the Word." I could have easily written: "In the beginning was love."

This is what we have to share with the world. When Jesus looked at the crowds of hurting, lost, broken, even captive people, He had compassion on them (Matt. 9:36). The mission of the church begins in compassion. In a world torn by competing and conflicting ideologies, partisan politics, hatred, and racism, we are in desperate need of the love of God that is found in Christ. It is a summons to a real change not born in legislation, policies, and agendas, but rather birthed in the human heart by the presence of Christ and proved by the preference of the poor. Jean Vanier predicted that a renaissance is coming to the church, where multitudes of communities will be founded on adoration and presence to the poor.[10]

Once church leaders learn again the theological link between lifting the poor and Christian spirituality, this renaissance will flourish. In beholding the poor, we are beholding Jesus; and when praying for the poor, we are praying the heart of Jesus.

11

SPECIAL SEASONS
OF PRAYER

Prayer is inspired by God in the depth of our
own nothingness.

—THOMAS MERTON[1]

There is another key that opens up divine doors that is
based on a simple fact: not all seasons are the same.
There are some days in our lives and ministries that
simply require more prayer and greater prayer intensity
than others. Mature Christians have learned to recognize
the seasons when the Lord is calling them to cancel their
schedules and come to the throne of God.

Solemn Assemblies

Special-called seasons of prayer are not new to the
Christian church. They actually gain their traction from
the Old Testament. One such special-called prayer gathering that is written of no less than fifteen times was the

holy convocation. Its first mention is in Exodus 12:16, where the first day and the seventh day of each Passover festival was to be reserved for a holy convocation. During these days, no work was to be done and everyone was to adhere to the altered diet of yeast-less bread. Another special-called gathering for prayer was the solemn assemblies, which is referred to nine times in the Old Testament. Joel 1:1 is one such example where the prophet told the people to sanctify a fast, call a solemn assembly, and gather the elders and all the people into the house of the Lord to cry before Him. These were to be sober events because they were nothing short of an appointment with God, usually during dark times. There were a couple instances in Israel's history when they came into a solemn assembly in a trite and perfunctory manner, and drew a rebuke from the prophets in Isaiah 1:13 and Amos 5:21. Through both prophets, God told how He despised and hated those insincere gatherings and, in fact, the incense they offered during the prayer ceremony smelled bad to Him. All to say, holy convocations and solemn assemblies were to be sober moments between a people and their God.

In the New Testament one only has to look at the life of Christ to see many special-called breakaways for prayer that He engaged in personally and with His disciples. The most famous was the night Jesus led the disciples into the garden of Gethsemane for a clandestine prayer meeting in Matthew 26:36–44. While most leaders would deem the evening as a prayer-meeting failure (because the disciples slept through most of the prayer moments), it was a special-called prayer gathering that Jesus arranged during a time of great spiritual darkness.

The book of Acts church naturally followed Jesus' example and during their challenging moments, they, too, called gatherings for prayer. Acts 4:31 tells of one such prayer meeting right after some of their leaders had been threatened by the authorities to be quiet, but as they prayed, a spirit of boldness swept into the prayer room with such force that the walls were shaken. Whether you call them holy convocations, solemn assemblies, prayer meetings, or weeks of prayer and fasting, these special-called gatherings for sober prayer are a significant part of the heritage of God's people and serve the purpose of regaining an upper hand during the day of trouble.

Mission that is fueled by prayer has been made quite clear to this point. However, special seasons of prayer and discernment are vital to ministry. The rhythm of the church calendar moves us from various focal points of the gospel and the mission of the church. I am watching with joy as people from non-liturgical traditions discover the cadence of the various church seasons and I find myself in relationships where I am coaching folks on the varied emphasis of a specific church season.

Lent and Advent are specific times of repentance and self-reflection in terms of our relationship with God. They offer a focus to recalculate and realign our lives toward God. Christmas and Easter are a celebration of our redemption drawing nigh, coming near. Epiphany and Pentecost are focused on mission and manifestation of the kingdom of God in the world.

Before you do anything new, launch a new ministry objective, or initiate a new mission effort, begin by laying a foundation of prayer. This prayer foundation is essential and calls a community together to invest their intercessions for wisdom and guidance as you move forward. Corporate prayer, solemn assemblies, and gathering for intercession not only lead to breakthrough, but also build unity in the ecclesia.

There are other times when God draws our attention and we become aware of an opportune moment. The terrorist attack on 9/11 was such a time where we were given an occasion to pray into that moment as a nation and pray for those who suffered.

Jesus' Prayer Retreats

While I've already mentioned Jesus' special-called prayer meeting in the garden, it is valuable for us to consider the many prayer retreats that He directed. One in particular that I find intriguing is in Mark 6:30–32, where John the Baptist had just been beheaded and Jesus took His disciples out of the fray of ministry to go to a deserted place on the other side of the lake. This prayer retreat was obviously for reasons of restoration—to provide space to deal with their grief over John's martyrdom. Though their season of quietude was cut short because the people ran around the lake and interrupted them, Jesus was saying something very important by this action: rest is an important part of warfare. In this era when fifty pastors a day are leaving the ministry, many for reasons of burnout, it is important to meditate upon Jesus' prayer retreats. When He felt tired, He pulled away to pray; when He saw His guys getting tired, He pulled them away to pray.

There is a need for more of Jesus' versions of prayer retreats in the body of Christ, especially among those who are on the frontlines of evangelism. I find it frustrating that groups who are often the best at planning prayer retreats are not contending for souls; and those who are living on the white-hot edge of evangelism are not the ones planning prayer retreats. This imbalance needs to be repaired, because the kingdom of God needs every servant on the frontlines and the kingdom of God needs His servants to be rested enough to open big doors for the inbreaking kingdom.

While this is seldom spoken of, human energy is needed to release divine energy upon the earth. I have noticed that my faith ebbs and flows with my physical energy level. I wish I were a greater man of God, but that is the raw truth. Jesus realized the same thing about His humanity and certainly His disciples' humanity. With pastoral counselors now diagnosing much of clergy burnout in terms of "exhaustion" and "exhaustion depression," we would do well to consider rest-oriented prayer retreats in our gospel battle plans. Rescuing the lost is unarguably the mission, but human hands turning keys in big doors require human energy. So, may the prayer for rest become tethered to the prayer for souls.

The pace of life is faster, more hectic, and more intense than ever before. For many of us, the demands on our time and the pressures we face are incredible.

In recent years, we have added an ever-present torrent of distraction: smartphone screens; news that comes in marked, character-numbered snippets; and a constant flurry of electronic data.

I sense a felt loss among many of my friends and colleagues. If we are not careful, our activity and distractions keep us from what is really important, life-giving, and eternal. I think the ancient art of *retreat* is all the more needed today in our hectic and distracted world. We desperately need to get away from our normal routines, finding time to be quiet and still, to reflect, and to reconnect with God through silence and prayer.

Jesus modeled this ancient discipline for us, regularly pulling away from the activity of the crowds and the disciples to be by Himself. He was not just by Himself, of course. Jesus sought solitude to spend time with His Father in heaven. In the sixth chapter of Mark, Jesus invites His disciples to do the same. After the brisk pace of ministry, they were feeling somewhat harassed and hurried, maybe a little tattered around the edges. Jesus wanted to lead them to something we all need: time away in quiet reflection; time to rest and be with God. This is especially true for those involved in active ministry, which is invigorating and fulfilling, yet draining at the same time.

Jesus invites us today to follow Him in this discipline by making regular spiritual retreats. How often do you see people do this? When was the last time you got away to be still? The Psalms teach us to "Be still, and know that I am God" (Ps. 46:10). I have found in my life that if

I am not still, I will not know God. But knowing God is what this earthly pilgrimage is all about.

I do not mean to say that our daily work is unimportant, or that we cannot find God in our everyday callings. The Christian life is multifaceted. There are many tasks set before us: evangelism, discipleship, stewardship, missions, justice, and repentance. On top of that there's paying bills, grocery shopping, getting the car repaired, and school functions. All of this work is important, even essential. The kingdom of God grows from work. But it is crucial to ask: Is our work centered in a heart that is in communion with the Lord? Does it flow from that center? I find that our work can be done in three postures:

Rushing: We are often so busy, running from work to school and shuttling our families to activities. It can be frantic, and we get lost in the process. We handle a variety of media streams that invade our lives with stress and distraction. We are often running so fast that we miss the more valuable moments of eternal import.

Rusting: We get stuck in the same routine, going through the motions day after day. It feels like movement, but we are getting nowhere. Life becomes monotonous, an endless routine leaving us empty and without purpose. We get stuck in a cycle, not aware that decades have gone by and we have not grown in our faith, relationships, and understanding.

Resting: From a position of rest, we become more keenly focused and are able to navigate life with a sense of calling and trust. Jesus never ran anywhere. He walked.

Yes, He grew weary at times, but because He knew the art of retreat, He would find moments of silence and solitude in each day. When we function from a posture of rest, we can work with greater efficiency and make progress in things that really matter.

How can we find this posture of rest in our everyday working lives? After more than thirty-five years of vocational ministry, I (Jon) have learned the importance of filling the core of my being with the restfulness that comes only from taking time to be with the Lord. You have probably heard sayings like "You cannot give away what you do not have," or "You cannot lead people to a place you have not been," or, my favorite, "You teach what you know but you reproduce what you are." These sayings are true! If I want to see my family, my workplace, and my community growing in their knowledge of the Lord, it means I need to have that at the center of my piety. To pray, read, study, focus, and be still, entering a time of solitude when I'm filled with the fruits and gifts of the Holy Spirit, is how I become a better priest, pastor, husband, father, and friend.

That is why twice a year for a week, I escape to a hermitage on retreat. I've been doing this for the past twenty years. When I go on retreat, I learn again a new rhythm and pattern of life. I hear a new cadence and, in doing so, I tune myself into my relationship with God. His voice becomes clearer, His presence sweeter, and my faith is fanned into a greater flame. It's a little like turning the lens on a blurry camera, bringing life back into proper focus. Retreat for me is a time of gathering spiritual fuel for every day. It brings me into a posture of rest, in which I can trust in God's work and fret less about my work. Doing this away moment regularly allows me to carry back into the everyday this posture of stillness. Knowing the hermitage journey, I am able to replicate the experience in a fifteen-minute walk or an hour-long sit and be still. I can hear the melody of retreat and it bids to me to slow down and listen. Whether at the hermitage or at my home, I can sing the familiar tune of almighty God beckoning me deeper into His felt presence.

A friend told me about a conversation with a member of his congregation. This woman had a dream. She was in heaven with Jesus, and as she looked around, she saw what looked like our planet at a distance. It was covered with black dots moving hurriedly all over, looking like ants swarming about. She asked Jesus: "What is that?"

Jesus replied: "It's my people doing all the things I never asked them to do."

Busyness and distraction of our culture has put us in danger of losing what is truly important. We need to reconnect with what will bring comprehensive healing and wholeness to our broken, distracted, and unfocused lives; to reunite body, soul, mind, and strength in God. I invite you to discover the power of personal retreat. I challenge you to find a place. Maybe it's a retreat center or a hermitage, or just a swing in your backyard, an open church chapel, or a city park where you can spend an hour in prayer and reflection. Wherever you find it, learn the art of retreat, of being still and entering into solitude and prayer. In doing so, you will gain the posture of restful trust that you need for taking on the work and the challenges of the missional journey God calls us all to travel.

This Kind

The disciples were frustrated. They had been released by Jesus to minister on their own and were having remarkable success in destroying the works of the devil, until that day. A young boy was being demonized and the father brought the boy to the disciples. They prayed over the child, expecting to reverse the darkness just like they had numerous times before. But for some reason, nothing happened. The boy foamed at the mouth and rolled around on the ground and was not helped at all by the disciples' prayers. When Jesus arrived, He healed the boy straightway, and the disciples' ministry confidence slumped. Afterward, they pulled Jesus aside and asked why their prayers had not worked. Mark 9:29 records Jesus' simple but profound answer: "This kind can come out by nothing but prayer and fasting." Every now and again, every leader and every church is going to come across "this kind." Some works of darkness are simply more rooted into the lives of its victims, and extra strength is required on the part of those who are confronting it. It is interesting that Jesus did not exclude Himself from this insight—as though the Son of God would be exempt. He simply stated that the *only thing* that plunders this kind of strongman was extra prayer and extra fasting, both of which Jesus had engaged in prior, more than the disciples had.

Fasting is both sacrificial and practical. It is sacrificial in that it tells the flesh no so as to tell the Spirit yes. And it is practical in that the time scheduled to eat can now be used for seeking God's interventions. Thus, fasting brings about the goal of John 3:30, that we must decrease so He may increase. Fasting intentionally weakens the flesh so as to give a greater portion of the Lord's power in us—the greater power we need to open some larger doors in heaven for some larger needs upon earth. For every church that is on the frontlines of evangelism, there will come a time when they face "this kind." It is at this moment they will find themselves in need of a special-called season of fasting and prayer. This is their Christian heritage. They will arise in power; they will dethrone the strongman. That is always the end of the story.

The Prayer That Turns the Tide

My father-in-law was a great Christian leader right up to the end of his life. Among the numerous pearls of wisdom he offered me through the years, the one I found most interesting was: "When you are facing a resistance in your ministry, bear down on that thing until it breaks." He went on to tell me that at times he could feel a brick wall when he was preaching or praying or leading his churches, and if he would set his forehead like flint against that resistance, it would relent and the will of God would overtake the moment and turn the tide. These are sage words from a veteran man of God. I wonder if the idea of bearing down against a resistance or turning the tide is practiced anymore? James 4:7 suggests that we resist the enemy until he flees. I have to admit that I have ignored that approach to prayer for much of my life. I'm quite sure I am not alone.

Jesus needs us to know how to turn the tide in our prayers. He needs this from us so much that He will provide seasons that require us to practice these guttural forms of prayer. Barry Black, the chaplain of the US Senate liked the prayer, "Disturb us, O Lord, when we are too pleased with ourselves."[2] Disturbances are necessary to deepen and develop a determination in our prayers. These measured disturbances force us to impute more power into our prayer lives. And more power on our lips translates to more doors being opened in heaven, which translates into more of God's will being released upon the earth.

I (Verlon) previously shared about the legal action brought against us, and the financial destruction that followed. This evil wind caught us by surprise. We had become quite effective at plundering the strongman's house in our city and had been leading many people to Jesus every month at our dinner churches. However, it could not be said that powerful prayers were regularly being offered in our ranks. We had not been arrogant; we had just been busy doing the gospel. But we had slipped into autopilot. We had enough flow coming from heaven to sustain us in the day of ease, but not enough to sustain us in the day of "this kind." However, now we faced a darkness that we had not encountered before. It disturbed us, and it sobered us. I immediately called a week of prayer and fasting, and our people responded remarkably. During that week, we saw our need to develop a new prayer strategy that had the ability to keep up with our evangelism strategy. By the next week we were committing to prayer walks and daily prayers as an ongoing strategy. And, once again, our people responded powerfully, and the dark clouds soon lost their grip on us. The legal case against us started to crumble, truth started to exonerate us, our finances began to restore, and, most of all, we learned how to turn the tide. We had been strong builders of the kingdom, but now we were becoming powerful warriors of the kingdom.

On a personal note, my wife and I recognized a genuine lift in our spirits after the week of prayer. Upon reflection, there had been a low-level depression affecting us for quite some time. What I thought was age related, or tiredness, or the normal pastoral pressures, turned out to be oppression from the strongman. That still just makes me mad when I think of how much time elapsed under the cloud of a needless depression. But once we increased our boldness in prayer, the strongman fled just like James 4:7 says would happen. Our season of prayer turned the tide in many ways, both for our ministry and for us personally. And a new prayer skill was birthed in us for the next time we face "this kind."

12

THE NEEDFUL UNION OF TROWEL AND SWORD

How do I profit by abandoning myself passively to His will if I lack the strength of will to obey His commands?

—THOMAS MERTON[1]

Some people know how to build but don't know how to battle; some know how to battle but don't know how to build. Few have learned to do both. However, any church that wants to prevail on the frontlines of evangelism will need to wear the dual identities of builder and warrior.

Mitzvah

There are those in the body of Christ who have adopted an idea that sinners simply need to be prayed in. These groups are ignoring the work of the trowel altogether and sidestepping great portions of Christian history. We simply cannot talk about evangelism prayer without a willingness to engage in evangelism activities. *Mitzvah* is a Hebrew term that refers to a prayer in the form of a deed.[2] Jewish culture has always held a very close relationship between prayer and action, while Western culture has separated these ideas. A true Hebrew in Jesus' day would validate their actions by praying and prove the seriousness of a prayer by corresponding actions; they simply could not do one without the other. Prayer and action were mutually dependent ideas. We see this clearly in James 2:17 (NIV), where it reads that "faith by itself, if it is not accompanied by action, is dead."

The truth is, Jesus expects us to do the hard missiological work of entering the lives of lost people-circles in our town and bringing them to the Savior. He also expects us to use our prayer keys to open up heaven's door for God's rescue plans to flow upon the earth. When a group gets their missiology right, they will know it by the many conversions that begin to occur. Their evangelism efforts will become surprisingly effective. Their confidence in using the gospel trowel will soar. They will join the coveted 1 percent of churches who know how to reach the lost. And when a group gets their prayer strategy right, the enemy can do nothing to stop them. They will pray with power and boldness. They will prayer walk their way from one lost neighborhood to the next. They will fill their entire city with the gospel like the Acts church did. We are not just people of powerful prayer; we are also people of powerful gospel action.

Piety is a church word that has fallen by the wayside. According to the Cambridge English Dictionary, it means a strong belief in God or a religion, shown by your worship and behavior. It is a marriage between belief and practice. Culturally, it can have a negative connotation as being religiously proud, even pharisaical. But let us reclaim the original intent. We are to be a pious people; fully devoted to God and living a transformed life by the things we do. Our work and actions are to flow from being saturated in God's presence. This picture of the trowel and sword is anchored in the theology of piety.

Trowels of the Next Era

It is interesting to note that Nehemiah and his men had to learn to use the trowel, even before they learned about the sword. How good are we at using the trowel? While previously mentioned, it bears repeating that only 1 percent of US churches across all denominational lines are growing as a result of reaching the lost.[3] Even though there are churches that have numerous hands raised during an altar call at the end of a sermon, it is more likely they are the dechurched and the prodigals coming back to faith than the secular lost coming to Christ for the first time. Don't get me wrong: anyone making their way back to Jesus is wonderful. But the American church's inability to expand the kingdom into the secular lost is devastating to all mathematical models of the future of the church. Our need to grow in the effective use of the gospel trowel is reaching a point of desperation in most denominations. For effective evangelism to arise, we need to acknowledge our obsession with the proclamation-event form of church, and willingly pursue other ways of doing church. I predict that the groups who are willing to do church in a way that matches the sociologies of the lost rather than continuing to do church in ways that match the sociologies of the already saved will usher in the trowels of the next era.

In this post-Christendom time, we need a pre-Christendom model that looks more like the ministry of Jesus and the church in the book of Acts. Just as Nehemiah ventured from being the cupbearer to the king and found himself the leader of a construction project, we must adapt to the changing landscape where we are living. Adaptation is necessary and this will require a reorientation of our efforts and resources toward a more authentic mission of going where the lost reside. There was a day, when people got in trouble, they would turn to the church. That day has passed for the most part. People are going to other outlets to address what foundationally is a spiritual need. Jesus calls us to go and be with them as salt and light.

When Effective Evangelism Meets Strategic Prayer

Nehemiah's story reveals the needful union between using a trowel to build the kingdom and using a sword to war against the enemy's attacks. Any group that decides to summon a Nehemiah-like spirit and commit to stop at nothing to reach the lost in their neighborhood will discover a trowel that fits their call. And as they continue to effectively use that trowel, they will start to experience new kinds of resistance rising up against them. Soon it will become clear that the strongman is trying to kick in their front door and threaten their future. It is then they must figure out how to use their sword.

Previously, such a church might have been able to pretend that evil was simply a spiritual path to be avoided. But after actually meeting the strongman and observing his intentional strategy against a frontlines church, confronting evil can no longer be avoided. The strongman's attacks might come in the form of financial depletion, relational conflict, burnout, or any number of dark attempts to suppress the people of God who are on mission. This is when a church either wilts back into passive safe-zones or boldly bursts forth to plunder the strongman more than ever. These are the moments that meek believers become lions and church attenders become warriors. Good missiology will show a group how to use a trowel and win the lost, but it takes an attack from the strongman to show a group how to pick up the sword of prayer and swing it with authority.

In many ways, it is availing ourselves of all the tools God gives us. I have learned in my limited work in carpentry and other construction initiatives that having the right tools is essential. There are unique tools that will craft and create something and make the process easier. I have from time to time found myself using the wrong tool, and it is difficult or ultimately does not work and may even break what I am working on. So it would be with sword-and-trowel prayers. By the Holy Spirit I discern what the situation is and what is needed. Some instances will call for prayers of deliverance and spiritual warfare; some will need prayers of encouragement; others, prayers for healing or provision. The mature Christian becomes proficient in discerning the circumstance. More so just as with other tools, the more you use them, the more skilled you become. As we engage in the gospel mission we get better at this work.

I am reminded about David. He had volunteered to take on Goliath and they tried to put King Saul's armor on him, but it did not fit. So instead, David took what he knew—his sling and a few rocks. I love this exchange:

> Saul replied, "You are not able to go out against this Philistine and fight him; you are only a young man, and he has been a warrior from his youth." But David said to Saul, "Your servant has been keeping his father's sheep. When a lion or a bear came and carried off a sheep from the flock, I went after it, struck it and rescued the sheep from its mouth. When it turned on me, I seized it by its hair, struck it and killed it. Your servant has killed both the lion and the bear; this uncircumcised Philistine will be like one of them, because he has defied the armies of the living God. The LORD who rescued me from the paw of the lion and the paw of the bear will rescue me from the hand of this Philistine." Saul

said to David, "Go, and the LORD be with you."
(1 Sam. 17:33–37 NIV)

Past experiences can help us in each step of this missional journey. God will use previous chapters to equip us for mission and ministry. David was confident in taking on Goliath because he had already defeated a lion and a bear. We gain both skill and proficiency in the practice. I became a musician, a preacher, a teacher, a photographer, all by practice. I also became a proficient person of prayer by praying.

Pastor and author Mark Batterson said that prayer is for when we reach the line between what we can do and what God can do. When a church stares into the steely eyes of the strongman, they are at that line where they need a powerful God to burst out of heaven with fire in His eyes and fight for them. It is then and only then that a church truly learns the difference between relational-appeal prayers and expectant-declarative prayers. Relational prayers edify the believer, but persistent, fervent, declarative prayers make the enemy flee as heaven's doors fling open and divine interventions burst forth.

Prayer Strategy Examples

Seasoned groups who serve on the frontlines of evangelism know well the value of choosing a prayer strategy to flank their soul-winning strategy. I remember reading of an evangelist from the last century who would send a forerunner to a city to pray. This front man would pray in that city until he felt that a spiritual freedom had been gained. Though his prayer work may take many months to achieve, he would continue until he sensed in his spirit that the price had been prayed for the gospel to flow freely into that city. He would then wire the evangelist that it was time for him to come. When the evangelist arrived, his meetings quickly brought about a significant harvest of souls. This was their prayer strategy, and it paired well with their evangelism strategy.

In this century, international evangelist Ed Silvoso has spoken fluently about the prayer strategy used for their crusades in South America. Evangelist Jack Dennison also has spoken about his prayer strategies in reaching large cities. I find particular interest, however, in the prayer strategy employed by Luis Palau's team as they get a city ready for one of their festivals. First, they have every church in the city designate a prayer leader for their church to pull together a prayer team from their church. Second, they schedule several corporate prayer events for twelve months leading up to a Palau event. Third, they schedule individuals and prayer teams offering 24/7 continuous prayer for forty days prior to the event. Fourth, they set a specific goal of praying for lost people by name (example: the festival in Eugene, Oregon, posted a prayer goal to have one thousand believers praying for five thousand unbelievers by name). Fifth, they sign up large numbers of intercessors to be praying during the hours the festival is occurring.[4]

The prayer strategy for the Fresh Expressions US movement is of equal interest. Fresh Expressions is planting thousands of new faith communities among lost people in ways that fit their sociologies. The prayer strategy they need is an ongoing approach rather than an event approach like Palau's team. Their prayer arm is called the Ananias Project and consists of three prayer approaches. First, they host Ananias Retreats, which are weekend events designed to train people in the skills of intercession. Second, they install their trained intercessors into a global prayer network from around the world who focus daily prayers and need-based responsive prayers specifically on the spread of Fresh Expression churches in the United States. Third, they organize prayer encounters that occur during national and regional conferences and intercede throughout the training sessions as well offering one-on-one anointing prayer for leaders and plant teams before they head for home.[5] I helped lead a Fresh Expressions Ananias Retreat this past year. It was a time of waiting, listening, and being still in a community of people all pressing into this prayer focus. Out of that concentrated time of prayer the Holy Spirit was made manifest in prophetic words, healing, anointing, and calling people into mission. People stepped out for the first time in the power of the Holy Spirit and were equipped in a deeper and more profound way to bear witness to Christ.

For our (Verlon's) dinner churches in Seattle, we chose to employ four prayer strategies. First, we use special-called solemn assemblies on an as-needed basis that are usually for a week in duration and include fasting and gathered corporate prayer events. Second, we use neighborhood prayer walks to usher in Christ's presence, in which each of our people have adopted one of the neighborhoods where we have a dinner church location and do a prayer walk singularly or with others every few weeks as their schedule allows.

Third, we pause daily for what we refer to as "It's Five O' Clock Somewhere," in which all of our people stop what they are doing at 5:00 p.m. every day and ask the Lord to pour into the dinner churches that are starting right then, and ask for Jesus to reveal Himself to the people that are in our rooms that night. This form of daily prayer is similar to the prayer pattern of the first church where they stopped to pray for the growth of the gospel whenever the Roman praetorian bell sounded to signal the time of day.[6] We realized we needed a prayer strategy that flowed with common reminders and daily rhythms to keep our people focused and praying; the five o'clock hour has become our praetorian bell.

And, fourth, the backbone of our prayer strategy is the weekly prayer gathering. We do this on Wednesday nights when all of our leadership teams come together, worship together, look into the Scriptures together, engage in a variety of corporate prayers together, and seek God for breakthroughs together. On these nights we expect to open some doors in heaven that were not open to us before we met. This weekly prayer gathering has become the heartbeat of our church; we pray favor into our story on Wednesdays and reap the benefits of that new favor throughout the rest of the week in all of our dinner church congregations. And the next Wednesday we gather to do it again. Years from now, we are quite sure that these Wednesday nights will be credited as the greatest reason we were able to advance the gospel into our city and our story.

Finding a Fit

We have been given many keys to open the doors of heaven and usher divine interventions onto the earth. I have identified thirty-three different evangelism-advancing prayer practices in this book, which are listed for clarity's sake in appendix 1. While I am sure no church is going to use all of these prayer keys, some strategic choices need to be made for any group wanting to prevail on the frontlines of evangelism. As previously stated, while we know dozens of different prayer practices that pair with evangelism, we only use four of them in our Seattle strategy.

So how do you choose a prayer strategy that is right for your story? Here are a few guidelines:

First, it is okay to say no to certain prayer practices even though they are in the Bible. Before you can say yes to the particular few that match your calling, you are going to need to say many nos. Christians often feel obligated to use everything in Scripture and everything that seems spiritual. This is a mistake. You have been sent to reach a particular social circle, so you will be best served by a few particular prayer practices.

Second, every group needs to adopt a set of prayer practices that align with their evangelism strategy. Once your group knows that they are sent to reach a particular people, a particular manner of reaching them will emerge. This is the apostolic nature of the church: to see different ways of reaching different people. Similarly, different prayer practices that pair well with their evangelism strategies are needed. The Spirit will help your group identify the prayer approaches that best empower your evangelism efforts. Ask for that insight. Certain prayer-forms will just seem right. Your group will feel power flowing from certain prayer approaches as they do it. So, enfold those prayer-forms into your strategy.

Third, find prayer practices that are potent enough to turn the tide in your evangelism calling. Many people pray, but some pray with authority and power. Look for the prayer practices that seem to open doors for your ministry, similar to book of Acts prayer meetings. I am not talking about a loud, boisterous corporate prayer meeting that would make a Pentecostal proud; it could be a quiet, small-group prayer meeting, but it releases divine power and watches resistant walls fall before them.

Fourth, develop approaches to prayer that flow with your group's natural rhythms. If your prayer strategy is too hard, it will break down over time. Some prayer practices that are natural to some churches are not to others. Look for prayer practices that have daily reminders like the praetorian bell, and clicks with your church's mindset. It might not be a prayer-form other churches use, but if it inspires your people to pray powerful prayers and contend for the souls in your neighborhood, then own it as your strategy. When all is said and done, the divine interventions that come to earth will not do so when God calls for it as much as when you and your people start calling for it.

Fifth, be open, listen, lean in, meditate on God's Word, worship, share in the sacraments, join your voice with others, wait with expectation, and ministry will flow. You will be prompted by the Holy Spirit to go, give, serve, engage, proclaim, connect, interact, and be present with people where they are. We come back to Luke 10: "The harvest is truly great, but the laborers are few; therefore, pray to the Lord of the harvest to send out laborers into His harvest" (v. 2). So raise your hand, sign up, volunteer, join prayer meetings in progress, and by all means, say, "Here I am, Lord, send me!" (see Isaiah 6:8).

A Beautiful Rhythm

When a group becomes equally proficient at using the trowel and the sword, a beautiful season of effectiveness sweeps into the life of the church. They are now going back and forth between two meaningful spiritual tasks: rescuing the perishing and ushering Christ into their neighborhoods. Wow, what a mission! And there is beauty in the mutuality of it. Thomas Merton talks about this divine interplay by saying, "Music is pleasing not only because of the sound but because of the silence that is in it: without the alternation of sound and silence there would be no rhythm."[7] There is a rhythmic beauty between effective evangelism and bold prayer. Oh, that the church of America would learn the rhythms of doing church for the lost and contending for souls in prayer.

> Lord Jesus Christ, you stretched out your arms of love on the hard wood of the cross that everyone might come *within the reach of your saving embrace*[8]: So clothe us in your Spirit that we, reaching forth our hands in love, may bring those who do not know you to the knowledge and love of you; for the honor of your Name. *Amen.*[9]

CONCLUSION

While there are many Christians who are serious about their prayer life, we fear that the prayer-forms capable of advancing the gospel into dark places are under-practiced. In the absence of effective evangelism, many churches have turned inward, and their prayer lives have followed suit. For the Christ-followers who desire a meaningful spiritual life, prayer is a necessary discipline; but for those who desire to be effective in evangelism, prayer is a necessary strategy.

Simply stated, frontlines prayer is different. While there are myriad of scriptures that teach evangelism-prompting prayer, there are a few watershed verses that underscore this difference more directly. One is found in Hebrews 11:6: "He is a rewarder of those who diligently seek Him." Another one is in James 5:16: "The effective, fervent prayer of a righteous man avails much." And still another verse on this theme is in Matthew 7:7: "Ask and it will be given to you, seek and you will find, knock and it will be opened to you." Yet another is about the persistent widow in Luke 18, who just would not stop knocking until the judge ruled in her favor. These cornerstone verses reveal a couple of undeniable truths about frontlines prayer.

First, there is an association between our fervency and God's response! We may not appreciate the persistence that the Lord is requesting from His saints, but the

Godhead sure appreciates it. In fact, they obviously like seeing the saints become passionate about what is needed and for what we are seeking from God.

Second, we tend to get what we pray for! When we pray with passion, things start to happen. However, the reverse is also true. If we do not muster fervent prayers, then answers do not flow our direction. This then brings me to a watershed question: For what are you seeking from God? In your life, in your family, in your church, in your city, in our nation? This is a repeating question I ask our prayer gathering in Seattle almost every week. I now direct this poignant question to you. Until we know what we are seeking God for, we will be fighting sleep during our prayer meetings rather than fighting to advance the kingdom. But once we know what we must seek for, then our prayer gatherings become punctuated with fervency, boldness, and the expectation that big doors are going to open for us! For what are you seeking from God?

The strongman has been comfortable leaving much of the American church alone in our buildings, where we only influenced each other. But that was yesterday. Today, there are a growing number of churches leaving the safety of their buildings and pouring out to the frontlines to reach their unchurched neighbors. It is a beautiful reversal of the "come to us" message that has dominated recent decades. Church groups are starting to go out to other neighborhoods and do church for those neighbors in ways that are true to their sociology. In this way, more and more Christians are locating the front-lines of evangelism in their towns and learning to become effective there. However, such a shift will predictably drive the need for these frontline Christians to become well-practiced at praying powerful prayers that open big doors in heaven. And the kind of prayer they used for growing their faith is not the kind of prayer they now need to contend for souls and change neighborhoods. The kind of prayers they used for building their ministry are not the kinds of prayer that they now need to stay on the frontlines. But know this: everyone who has been called to join the God-family rescue business has been divinely outfitted with the necessary weapons to prevail.

My (Verlon's) first position in ministry was serving as a youth pastor in Bend, Oregon. The first day on the job I was handed a huge ring of keys on a retractable belt-clip. Those were the days when master keys were not common, so I literally needed twenty-five different keys to navigate freely through that building. Almost every door had a different key; there were so many keys on that retractor that they were creating wear patterns on all of my pants after only a few months. But that over-sized ring of keys serves as a great picture for us.

Every servant who is on the frontlines of evangelism has been given a ring of keys too—all of which open big doors in heaven. The question is: Do we know that we have them? Please hear me when I say that the Lord has given you many prayer keys and He expects you to use them. This fact should inspire great confidence in us and lead us to pray like we know something significant is going to happen whenever we do it. Pray like you mean it. Use your keys with authority. Contend for souls. Change your neighborhood. There is not a single reason in heaven or on earth why you cannot open big doors and usher the kingdom of God right into your local story. The keys are already in your pocket!

APPENDIX 1

Following is an overview of the different prayer keys that have been given to those who are serving on the frontlines of evangelism and that have been discussed in these chapters. These prayers and prayer practices have the capacity to move the hand of God, contend for souls, and change ministries.

Overview of Prayer Keys

- Key #1: Acknowledge the War
- Key #2: Commit to the Family Rescue Business
- Key #3: Here Am I, Send Me!
- Key #4: A Burden for the Lost
- Key #5: Wait upon the Lord
- Key #6: Weeping and Mourning
- Key #7: Groanings
- Key #8: Travailing Prayer
- Key #9: The Fervent, Persistent, Tenacious, Bold Prayer
- Key #10: Boldly Attack the Enemy
- Key #11: Quote God's Words
- Key #12: The Name of Jesus
- Key #13: Presencing Worship
- Key #14: Disinvite/Invite Prayers
- Key #15: Corporate Prayer for Evangelism
- Key #16: Open Heaven's Door
- Key #17: Submission to Kingdom Plans

- Key #18: Neighborhood Prayer Walks
- Key #19: Praying in the Spirit
- Key #20: Breathe Blessing
- Key #21: Here, Lord, Here
- Key #22: Broken for the Helpless
- Key #23: Lean upon Mercy
- Key #24: Confronting Injustice
- Key #25: Calling on the Provider
- Key #26: Cooperating with the Constant Flow
- Key #27: Solemn Assemblies
- Key #28: "This Kind" Prayers
- Key #29: Fasting
- Key #30: Trowel and Sword
- Key #31: Answering God's Prayers
- Key #32: Rhythmic Daily Prayers
- Key #33: Contend for Souls!

APPENDIX 2

Taken from *The Book of Common Prayer and Administration of the Sacraments and Other Rites and Ceremonies of the Church, Together with the Psalter or Psalms of David, According to the Use of the Episcopal Church* (New York, Church Publishing Incorporated, 1979).

THE GREAT LITANY

To be said or sung, kneeling, standing, or in procession; before the Eucharist or after the Collects of Morning or Evening Prayer; or separately; especially in Lent and on Rogation days.

O God the Father, Creator of heaven and earth,
Have mercy upon us.

O God the Son, Redeemer of the world,
Have mercy upon us.

O God the Holy Ghost, Sanctifier of the faithful,
Have mercy upon us.

O holy, blessed, and glorious Trinity, one God,
Have mercy upon us.

Remember not, Lord Christ, our offenses, nor the offenses of our forefathers; neither reward us according to our sins. Spare us, good Lord, spare thy people, whom

thou hast redeemed with thy most precious blood, and by thy mercy preserve us forever.
Spare us, good Lord.

From all evil and wickedness; from sin; from the crafts and assaults of the devil; and from everlasting damnation,
Good Lord, deliver us.

From all blindness of heart; from pride, vainglory, and hypocrisy; from envy, hatred, and malice; and from all want of charity,
Good Lord, deliver us.

From all inordinate and sinful affections; and from all the deceits of the world, the flesh, and the devil,
Good Lord, deliver us.

From all false doctrine, heresy, and schism; from hardness of heart, and contempt of thy Word and commandment,
Good Lord, deliver us.

From lightning and tempest; from earthquake, fire, and flood; from plague, pestilence, and famine,
Good Lord, deliver us.

From all oppression, conspiracy, and rebellion; from violence, battle, and murder; and from dying suddenly and unprepared,
Good Lord, deliver us.

By the mystery of thy holy Incarnation; by thy holy Nativity and submission to the Law; by thy Baptism, Fasting, and Temptation,
Good Lord, deliver us.

By thine Agony and Bloody Sweat; by thy Cross and Passion; by thy precious Death and Burial; by thy glorious Resurrection and Ascension; and by the Coming of the Holy Ghost,
Good Lord, deliver us.

In all time of our tribulation; in all time of our prosperity; in the hour of death, and in the day of judgment,
Good Lord, deliver us.

We sinners do beseech thee to hear us, O Lord God; and that it may please thee to rule and govern thy holy Church Universal in the right way,
We beseech thee to hear us, good Lord.

That it may please thee to illumine all [clergy and leaders] with true knowledge and understanding of thy Word; and that both by their preaching and living, they may set it forth, and show it accordingly,
We beseech thee to hear us, good Lord.

That it may please thee to bless and keep all thy people,
We beseech thee to hear us, good Lord.

That it may please thee to send forth laborers into thy harvest, and to draw all mankind into thy kingdom,
We beseech thee to hear us, good Lord.

That it may please thee to give to all people increase of grace to hear and receive thy Word, and to bring forth the fruits of the Spirit,
We beseech thee to hear us, good Lord.

That it may please thee to bring into the way of truth all such as have erred, and are deceived,
We beseech thee to hear us, good Lord.

That it may please thee to give us a heart to love and fear thee, and diligently to live after thy commandments,
We beseech thee to hear us, good Lord.

That it may please thee so to rule the hearts of thy servants, the President of the United States (or of this nation), and all others in authority, that they may do justice, and love mercy, and walk in the ways of truth,
We beseech thee to hear us, good Lord.

That it may please thee to make wars to cease in all the world; to give to all nations unity, peace, and concord; and to bestow freedom upon all peoples,
We beseech thee to hear us, good Lord.

That it may please thee to show thy pity upon all prisoners and captives, the homeless and the hungry, and all who are desolate and oppressed,
We beseech thee to hear us, good Lord.

That it may please thee to give and preserve to our use the bountiful fruits of the earth, so that in due time all may enjoy them,
We beseech thee to hear us, good Lord.

That it may please thee to inspire us, in our several callings, to do the work which thou givest us to do with singleness of heart as thy servants, and for the common good,
We beseech thee to hear us, good Lord.

That it may please thee to preserve all who are in danger by reason of their labor or their travel,
We beseech thee to hear us, good Lord.

That it may please thee to preserve, and provide for, all women in childbirth, young children and orphans, the widowed, and all whose homes are broken or torn by strife,
We beseech thee to hear us, good Lord.

That it may please thee to visit the lonely; to strengthen all who suffer in mind, body, and spirit; and to comfort with thy presence those who are failing and infirm,
We beseech thee to hear us, good Lord.

That it may please thee to support, help, and comfort all who are in danger, necessity, and tribulation,
We beseech thee to hear us, good Lord.

That it may please thee to have mercy upon all mankind,
We beseech thee to hear us, good Lord.

That it may please thee to give us true repentance; to forgive us all our sins, negligences, and ignorances; and to endue us with the grace of thy Holy Spirit to amend our lives according to thy holy Word,
We beseech thee to hear us, good Lord.

That it may please thee to forgive our enemies, persecutors, and slanderers, and to turn their hearts,
We beseech thee to hear us, good Lord.

That it may please thee to strengthen such as do stand; to comfort and help the weak-hearted; to raise up those who fall; and finally to beat down Satan under our feet,
We beseech thee to hear us, good Lord.

That it may please thee to grant to all the faithful departed eternal life and peace,
We beseech thee to hear us, good Lord.

That it may please thee to grant that, in the fellowship of [_____ and] all the saints, we may attain to thy heavenly kingdom,
We beseech thee to hear us, good Lord.

The Officiant concludes with the following or some other Collect.

Let us pray.

Almighty God, who hast promised to hear the petitions of those who ask in thy Son's Name: We beseech thee mercifully to incline thine ear to us who have now made our prayers and supplications unto thee; and grant that those things which we have asked faithfully according to thy will, may be obtained effectually, to the relief of our necessity, and to the setting forth of thy glory; through Jesus Christ our Lord. *Amen.*

NOTES

Chapter One: Prayer Billabongs

1. Thomas Merton, *No Man Is an Island* (New York: Houghton Mifflin Harcourt Publishing, 1955), 182.

2. Mark Batterson, *In a Pit with a Lion on a Snowy Day: How to Survive and Thrive When Opportunity Roars* (Colorado Springs, CO: Multnomah Books, 2006), 62, italics in original.

3. Michael Griffiths, *Shaking the Sleeping Beauty: Arousing the Church to Its Mission* (Leicester LE1, England: 1980), Prayer from *Didache* 10:5, 203.

4. Alan Roxburgh and Scott Boren, *Introducing the Missional Church: What It Is, Why It Matters, How to Become One* (Grand Rapids, MI: Baker Books, 2009), 94.

5. Adapted from *The Book of Common Prayer* 1979—The Burial of the Dead / Rite II, 491–500.

6. Timothy Keller, *Center Church: Doing Balanced, Gospel-Centered Ministry in Your City* (Grand Rapids, MI: Zondervan Publishing, 2012), 259.

7. Dan Kimball, *Emerging Worship: Creating Worship Gatherings for New Generations* (Grand Rapids, MI: Zondervan Publishers, 2004), 64.

8. Michael Slaughter and Warren Bird, *Unlearning Church: Just When You Thought You Had Leadership All Figured Out!* (Loveland, CO: Group Publishers, 2002), 162.

9. *The Book of Common Prayer and Administration of the Sacraments and Other Rites and Ceremonies of the Church, Together with the Psalter or Psalms of David, According*

to the Use of the Episcopal Church (New York: Church
Publishing Incorporated, 1979), 868.

Chapter Two: Effective Evangelism and the Subsequent War

1. Thomas Merton, *No Man Is an Island* (New York:
   Houghton Mifflin Harcourt Publishing, 1955), 197.
2. Jim Cymbala, "We Must Change Our Game Plan,"
   lecture to the General Council of the Assemblies of God,
   Orlando, FL, August 7, 2013.
3. Aubrey Malphurs, *Advanced Strategic Planning: A New
   Model for Church and Ministry Leaders* (Grand Rapids,
   MI: Baker Books, 2005), 24.
4. John Bishop, *Dangerous Church: Risking Everything
   to Reach Everyone* (Grand Rapids, MI: Zondervan
   Publishing, 2011), 39.
5. *The Book of Common Prayer and Administration of the
   Sacraments and Other Rites and Ceremonies of the Church,
   Together with the Psalter or Psalms of David, According
   to the Use of the Episcopal Church* (New York: Church
   Publishing Incorporated, 2015), 332, emphasis added.
6. See Billy Graham Association, https://www.nae.net
   /when-americans-become-christians/. Last accessed
   February 2021.

Chapter Three: A Simple Theology of Prayer

1. Thomas Merton, *No Man Is an Island* (New York:
   Houghton Mifflin Harcourt Publishing, 1955), 117.
2. James Emery White, *Serious Times: Making Your
   Life Matter in an Urgent Day* (Downers Grove, IL:
   InterVarsity Press, 2004), 86.
3. Eugene Peterson, Interview with *Christianity Today*'s
   Rodney Clapp, April 3, 1987.

4. Darrel Guder, *The Continuing Conversion of the Church* (Grand Rapids, MI: Eerdmans Publishing, 2000), 19.

Chapter Four: Inviting the Kingdom onto Earth

1. Thomas Merton, *No Man Is an Island* (New York: Houghton Mifflin Harcourt Publishing, 1955), 118.

2. M. Robert Mulholland Jr., *Invitation to a Journey: A Road Map for Spiritual Formation* (Downers Grove, IL: InterVarsity Press, 1993), 108.

3. Keith Long, *Room to Grow* (Peabody, MA: Hendrickson, 1999), quoted in *Men of Integrity* (3.2).

4. M. Robert Mulholland Jr., *Invitation to a Journey*, 166.

5. Robert Anderson, *Circles of Influence: Expanding Your Leadership Capabilities in the Church* (Chicago, IL: Moody Press, 1991), 22–23.

6. Dan Kimball, *They Like Jesus but Not the Church: Insights from Emerging Generations* (Grand Rapids, MI: Zondervan Publishing House, 2007), 47.

7. Ibid.

8. Charles Colson, *The Faith: What Christians Believe, Why They Believe It, and Why It Matters* (Grand Rapids, MI: Zondervan Publishers, 2008), 123.

9. Roger Heuser, "Soul Care," live lecture for an Assemblies of God Theological Seminary Doctor of Ministry Class held at Northwest University, Kirkland, WA, October 24, 2012.

10. Religion News Service Guest Commentary, September 15, 2008, https://religionnews.com/2008/09/15/guest-commentary-jesus-didnt-come-to-take-sides-he-came-to-take-over1/.

11. Richard Stearns, *The Hole in Our Gospel: What Does God Expect of Us? The Answer That Changed My Life*

and Might Just Change the World (Colorado Springs, CO: Thomas Nelson Publishers, 2010), 13.

Chapter Five: Focused on the Family Rescue Business

1. Thomas Merton, *No Man Is an Island* (New York: Houghton Mifflin Harcourt Publishing, 1955), 130–31.

2. John Bishop, *Dangerous Church: Risking Everything to Reach Everyone* (Grand Rapids, MI: Zondervan Publishing, 2011), 39.

3. David Benner, *Care of Souls: Revisioning Christian Nurture and Counsel* (Grand Rapids, MI: Baker Books, 1998), 37.

4. Leanne Van Dyk, *A More Profound Alleluia: Theology and Worship in Harmony* (Grand Rapids, MI: Eerdmans Publishing Co., 2005), 98.

5. John Ortberg quoted in Leonard Sweet, *Aqua Church 2.0: Piloting Your Church in Today's Fluid Culture* (Colorado Springs, CO: David C. Cook Publishers, 1999), 225.

6. Tom Clegg and Warren Bird, *Lost in America: How You and Your Church Can Impact the World Next Door* (Loveland, CO: Group Publishers, 2001), 121.

Chapter Six: Willing to Wait upon God

1. Thomas Merton, *No Man Is an Island* (New York: Houghton Mifflin Harcourt Publishing, 1955), 260.

2. Gordon Fee, *Paul, the Spirit, and the People of God* (Peabody, MA: Hendrickson Publishers, 1996), 149.

3. Jean Vanier, *Community and Growth* (Mahwah, NJ: Paulist Press, 1989), 16.

4. James White, *A Brief History of Christian Worship* (Nashville, TN: Abingdon Press, 1993), 70.

5. David Thomas, Presentation on "Prevailing Prayer," New Room Conference, Tulsa, OK, March 30, 2017.

Chapter Seven: The Historic Cry for Boldness

1. Thomas Merton, *No Man Is an Island* (New York: Houghton Mifflin Harcourt Publishing, 1955), 135.

2. Vince Antonucci, *I Became a Christian and All I Got Was This Lousy T-Shirt: Replacing Souvenir Religion with Authentic Spiritual Passion* (Grand Rapids, MI: Baker Books, 2008), 17.

3. Michael Slaughter and Warren Bird, *Unlearning Church: Just When You Thought You Had Leadership All Figured Out!* (Loveland, CO: Group Publishers, 2002), 160–61.

4. Tom Clegg and Warren Bird, *Lost in America: How You and Your Church Can Impact the World Next Door* (Loveland, CO: Group Publishers, 2001), 121.

5. Quoted in Dan Allender, *Leading with a Limp: Take Full Advantage of Your Most Powerful Weakness* (Colorado Springs, CO: WaterBrook Press, 2006), 77.

6. Warren Bennis, Thomas Cummings, and Gretchen Spreitzer, *The Future of Leadership: Today's Top Leadership Thinkers Speak to Tomorrow's Leaders* (San Francisco, CA: Jossey-Bass, 2001), 256.

Chapter Eight: Dispelling Darkness

1. Thomas Merton, *No Man Is an Island* (New York: Houghton Mifflin Harcourt Publishing, 1955), 254.

2. Henry M. Morris and Arnold Ehlert, *The Genesis Record: A Scientific and Devotional Commentary on the Book of Beginnings* (Grand Rapids, MI: Baker Books, 1976), 8.

3. See entry on Infant Jaundice; https://www.mayoclinic
   .org/diseases-conditions/infant-jaundice/diagnosis
   -treatment/drc-20373870#:~:text=Light%20therapy
   %20(phototherapy).,both%20the%20urine%20and
   %20stool.

4. *The Book of Common Prayer and Administration of the
   Sacraments and Other Rites and Ceremonies of the Church,
   Together with the Psalter or Psalms of David, According
   to the Use of the Episcopal Church* (New York: Church
   Publishing Incorporated, 1979), 236.

5. James White, *A Brief History of Christian Worship*
   (Nashville, TN: Abingdon Press, 1993), 23.

6. Carl Raschke, *Globo-Christ: The Church and Postmodern
   Culture* (Ada, MI: Baker Academic, 2008), 134.

7. The Westminster Confession of Faith: *Shorter
   Catechism*.1. See https://prts.edu/wp-content/uploads
   /2016/12/Shorter_Catechism.pdf.

8. Robert Anderson, *Circles of Influence: Expanding Your
   Leadership Capabilities in the Church* (Chicago, IL:
   Moody Press, 1991), 322.

9. Darrell Guder, *Missional Church: A Vision for the Sending
   of the Church in North America* (Grand Rapids, MI:
   Eerdmans Publishing, 1998), 113.

Chapter Nine: The Unparalleled Power of Prayer Walks

1. Thomas Merton, *No Man Is an Island* (New York:
   Houghton Mifflin Harcourt Publishing, 1955), 108.

2. Steve Fry. Copyright by Deepfryed music, 1980.

3. Tom Clegg and Warren Bird, *Lost in America: How
   You and Your Church Can Impact the World Next Door*
   (Loveland, CO: Group Publishers, 2001), 121.

4. Chuck Lawless, *The Great Commission Resurgence: Fulfilling God's Mandate in Our Time* (Nashville, TN: B & H Publishing Group, 2010), 70–71.

5. Frederica Mathewes-Green, *The Church in Emerging Culture: Five Perspectives* (El Cajon, CA: Zondervan Publishing, 2003), 179.

6. D. A. Carson, *Christ and Culture Revisited* (Grand Rapids, MI: Eerdmans Publishing, 2008), 214.

Chapter Ten: The Least, the Last, and the Left Behind

1. Thomas Merton, *No Man Is an Island* (New York: Houghton Mifflin Harcourt Publishing, 1955), 21.

2. Ibid., 216.

3. Marva Dawn, *Reaching Out without Dumbing Down: A Theology of Worship for This Modern Time* (Grand Rapids, MI: Eerdmans Publishing Co., 1995), 265.

4. Craig Blomberg, *Neither Poverty nor Riches: A Biblical Theology of Possessions* (Downers Grove, IL: InterVarsity Press, 1999), 94.

5. Richard Stearns, *The Hole in Our Gospel: What Does God Expect of Us? The Answer That Changed My Life and Might Just Change the World* (Colorado Springs, CO: Thomas Nelson Publishers, 2010), 17.

6. Craig Blomberg, *Neither Poverty nor Riches*, 119.

7. Thomas Merton, *No Man Is an Island*, 169.

8. Desmond Tutu quoted in NT Wright live lecture @ Missio Alliance Conference, Alexandria, VA, April 30, 2017.

9. Richard Stearns, *The Hole in Our Gospel*, 60.

10. Jean Vanier, *Community and Growth* (Mahwah, NJ: Paulist Press, 1989), 63.

Chapter Eleven: Special Seasons of Prayer

1. Thomas Merton, *No Man Is an Island* (New York: Houghton Mifflin Harcourt Publishing, 1955), 43.
2. Barry Black, *From the Hood to the Hill: A Story of Overcoming* (Nashville, TN: Thomas Nelson Publishing, 2006), 219.

Chapter Twelve: The Needful Union of Trowel and Sword

1. Thomas Merton, *No Man Is an Island* (New York: Houghton Mifflin Harcourt Publishing, 1955), 16.
2. Michael Frost and Alan Hirsch, *The Shaping of Things to Come: Innovation and Mission for the Twenty-First Century Church* (Ada, MI: Baker Books, 2013), 142.
3. John Bishop, *Dangerous Church: Risking Everything to Reach Everyone* (Grand Rapids, MI: Zondervan Publishing, 2011), 39.
4. Randy Burtis, festival director for Luis Palau. Phone interview on July 9, 2017.
5. Cheryl McCarthy, director of the Ananias Project. Live interview on July 25, 2017.
6. Vince Antonucci, *I Became a Christian and All I Got Was This Lousy T-Shirt: Replacing Souvenir Religion with Authentic Spiritual Passion* (Grand Rapids, MI: Baker Books, 2008), 101.
7. Thomas Merton, *No Man Is an Island*, 127.
8. *The Book of Common Prayer and Administration of the Sacraments and Other Rites and Ceremonies of the Church, Together with the Psalter or Psalms of David, According to the Use of the Episcopal Church* (New York: Church Publishing Incorporated), 101, emphasis added.
9. Ibid., emphasis in original.

CPSIA information can be obtained
at www.ICGtesting.com
Printed in the USA
LVHW031324140222
710620LV00001B/2